• TASTE OF OLDHAM •

ADVICE TO A WIFE

Thou mun keep his whoam pleasant and sweet,
    An' everything fit to be seen;
Thou mun keep his hearth cheerful and breet,
    Thou mun keep thisel tidy and clean.
A good tempered wife will entice
    To a fireside that's cosy and trim;
Men liken to see their wives nice,
    And I'm sure that it's so with your Jim.
Thou mun hev his meals cooked to his mind,
    At the reet time, and dacently laid;
Tak' pains, an' thou'll very soon find
    How nice a plain dish can be made.
Good cooking keeps likin' alive,
    With a woman that's noan short o' wit,
An' there's never a craiter i'th hive
    But's fond of a toothsome tit-bit.

Edwin Waugh

• BY •

SHEILA TAYLOR

·ACKNOWLEDGEMENTS·

I should like to thank everyone who has been concerned in the preparation of this book. I thank those of my friends and colleagues who have been involved in many practical ways. In particular I thank Richard Lambert for his guidance and support, and Freda Millett, Peter Fox, Lilamani Woolrych and Jane Bonney for their professional expertise. I am especially grateful to my husband for his help in so many ways.

Recipes have been provided by local people. In particular I should like to thank Mrs. L. Bennett, Miss M. Buckley, Mrs. Ann Cox, Miss Illingworth, Mrs. Mugan, Mrs. Newton, Mrs. Smith, Mr. E. Taylor, Mrs. B. Watson and Mrs. Whitehead. Help has also been received from Clifford Wimpenny and Christine Bannister of Ferranti International, Philip Hirst of the "Oldham Evening Chronicle", and the staff of the Local History Library. Stefan and Nadia Moroz provided most of the information and recipes for the section on Ukrainian food.

The recipes are predominantly traditional ones. All prevalent health and safety precautions concerned with food preparation should be strictly adhered to.

I acknowledge copyright of material provided by Lilamani Woolrych, Ferranti International plc, Bovril Ltd., RHM Foods Ltd., Wander Ltd., New World Domestic Appliances Ltd., Ministry of Agriculture, Fisheries and Food, Department of Energy, Department of Employment. Government material is reproduced with the permission of the Controller of Her Majesty's Stationery Office.

PREFACE & CONTENTS

"Taste of Oldham" is a presentation of the growth of the town, along with its traditional food.

Oldham is a town with a history and tradition of thrift and hard work. The food is a reflection of its people and their lifestyle. The recipes have been collected from many sources; a number have been handed down over generations. They are presented as they were given to me, and to retain their individuality I have not put them into any standard format.

I hope that the book will evoke memories and also encourage a new generation to taste the food of their grandparents.

THE GROWTH OF OLDHAM

– CHAPTER ONE –

The Oldham of today is known as "the town in the countryside". Historical records show it to be a fairly accurate description. The village of Aldehulme is recorded sometime around 1180, and from Aldehulme developed the town of Oldham.

Hartley Bateson states, in his "History of Oldham", that during the seventeenth century, farming was the principal occupation. It was probably sheep farming, as references are found to the occupations of woollen draper, clothier and weaver.

The population of Oldham in 1714 was 1,732. About this time, Daniel Defoe made his journey through Great Britain, and wrote about the area ". . . we saw the houses full of lusty fellows, some at the dye vat, some at the loom, others dressing the cloths; the women and children carding and spinning; all employed from the youngest to the oldest . . . The people in general live long. They enjoy a good air, and under such circumstances hard labour is naturally attended with the blessing of health if not riches". Defoe's description carried a certain omen.

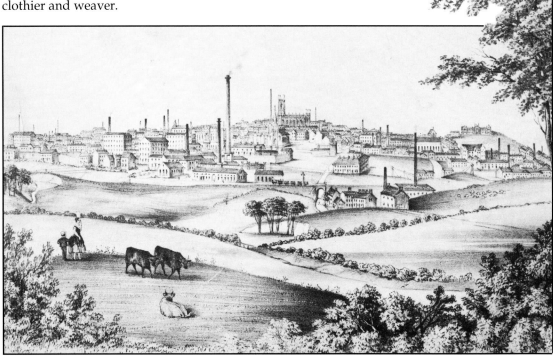

Oldham from Glodwick Fields, 1830.

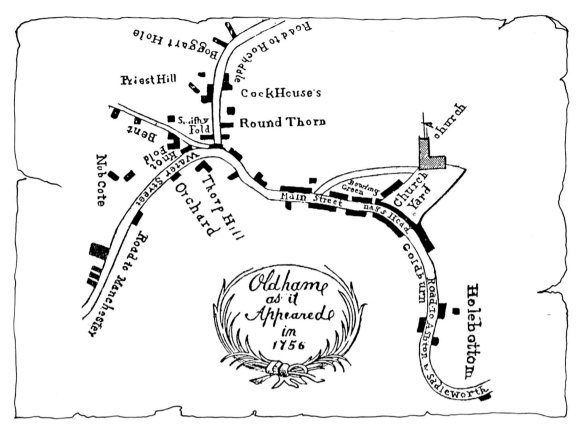

Probably the greatest change in the town's development occurred somewhere between 1750 and 1830, when what was little more than a village became a wealthy, prosperous town.

The Industrial Revolution brought about the change in the township, and the lifestyles of the residents, old and new. A combination of a developing transport system and the use of machinery were the two major factors in the evolution of Oldham as an industrial centre.

Initially, the roads around Oldham were few and probably badly constructed of stone, gravel and pebbles. An important means of communication was by canal, the two affecting Oldham being the Rochdale Canal and the Ashton Canal. These canals in their turn were later used to bring in more advanced road-building materials—setts, ashes and limestone, so communication by road could be improved.

The need for good communication was to enable the town to take advantage of the growth in the cotton industry. In the 1760's and early 1770's cotton spinning was largely a domestic industry, but with the invention of James Hargreaves' "Spinning Jenny", (about 1764) spinning was speeded up. Samuel Crompton invented his mule, in 1776, for spinning fine yarn. Richard Arkwright then developed the idea of bringing spinners together to work under one roof, and Oldham as a town of cotton mills came into being, from the late 1770's.

Such a transition, from a domestic industry to a factory system, in a comparatively short

Oldham—Tommyfield Market.

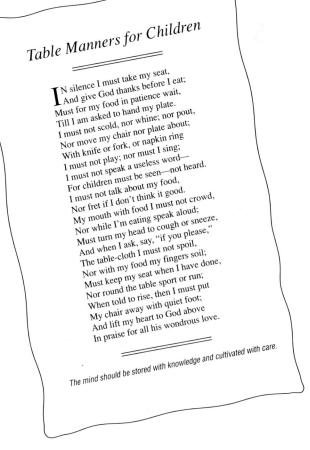

Table Manners for Children

IN silence I must take my seat,
And give God thanks before I eat;
Must for my food in patience wait,
Till I am asked to hand my plate.
I must not scold, nor whine; nor pout,
Nor move my chair nor plate about;
With knife or fork, or napkin ring
I must not play; nor must I sing;
I must not speak a useless word—
For children must be seen—not heard.
I must not talk about my food,
Nor fret if I don't think it good.
My mouth with food I must not crowd,
Nor while I'm eating speak aloud;
Must turn my head to cough or sneeze,
And when I ask, say, "if you please,"
The table-cloth I must not spoil;
Nor with my food my fingers soil;
Must keep my seat when I have done,
Nor round the table sport or run;
When told to rise, then I must put
My chair away with quiet foot;
And lift my heart to God above
In praise for all his wondrous love.

The mind should be stored with knowledge and cultivated with care.

time, meant a change in the lifestyles of the workers. From working at home (where domestic tasks fitted in with other work), women went out to work in factories, yet still had to provide food for their families.

The variety of food was not very great. Only a fairly small amount of food was produced locally, but it was supplemented by a greater variety brought by canal from the agricultural areas in Yorkshire.

The available ingredients determined the type of food which was cooked, and traditional local recipes are based on those ingredients.

A list of available common foods for 1802 shows "Meal, Flour, Malt, Treacle, Butter, Cheese, Pork, Beef, Mutton, Potatoes, Onions, Sugar, White Peas". Other records from this Industrial Revolution period show that as much use as possible was made of locally grown fruit. Mention is made of wimberries, gooseberries, damsons, plums, pears and "hazle-nuts". The corn-harvest was always a matter for concern, affecting the price of flour

and therefore the price of bread, and poor crops of peas, beans, cabbages or turnips could make a difference to the limited variety of food available to most of the population. Herbs such as sage and mint were grown, and dried for use in winter-time to enliven bland ingredients.

During this time, fluctuations in the cotton industry meant that there were times of great poverty for some families. One account, at the beginning of 1812 states "the old English hospitality is nearly extinguished in every family; for at this very time the lower class of people who have a family of small children are absolutely short of the common necessaries of life . . . Roast beef, pyes and ale are not to be met with at the poor man's table, but on the contrary, misery and want".

Another account, in 1826 describes how "in Oldham you will see great numbers parading the streets in a starving state, and numbers are rangeing the fields in search of nettles . . . or anything green, which they boil and mix with oatmeal, of which they make a hearty meal".

The "Annals of Oldham" for 1812 quote Lord Brougham who, in a speech said, "The food which now sustains them—the working classes—is of the lowest, and of that there is not nearly a sufficient supply; bread or even potatoes are out of the question, the luxuries of animal food or even milk they have long ceased to think of. A gentleman interested in the cotton trade went to collect his rents, and when he saw the tenants sitting down to a scanty dinner of oatmeal and water—their only meal in the twenty-four hours—he could not stand the sight and came away unable to ask for his rent".

However, there were times of celebration. The Napoleonic wars ended in 1814, and the Annals

© *Crown Copyright 1989.*

6

of Oldham tell that "public rejoicing took place in Oldham on Monday the 25th (of April), when all ranks of people manifested there joy on the downfall of Buonoparte. At an early hour the bells were ringing, the gentlemen of the town and neighbourhood walked in procession through the town . . . They were attended by a band of musick; they had a deal of flags and collors, with different devices on them . . . The gentlemen set down to a sumtious dinner at the Spread Eagle Inn . . . A sheep was roasted whole in the streets . . . the different manufacturers gave dinners and ale to their respective workpeople, who paraded the streets with musick and flags with different devices on. A pair of looms were drawn in a cart where a person was weaving callico, and a person representing Buonoparte was winding. Every degredation was used to insult the memory of the fallen monarch, whose tyrannical career was at an end. The whole was conducted with the greatest harmony and goodwill, ale &c. flowed in the greatest profusion".

Eat slowly and you will not over eat

Never quit a

Late at breakfast = hurried for dinner — cross at tea —

Lay loaded guns in safe places, and never imitate firing a gun in jest —

A short needle makes the most ... in plain sewing

Never leave saddle or draught horses, while in use, by ... nor go immediately

The poor man fasts because he has no meat, the sick man fasts because he will not eat, the miser fasts with greedy mind to spare, the glutton fasts to eat the greater share, the hypocrite will fast to seem more holy, the righteous man to punish sin and folly —

Little deeds are like seeds, they grow to flowers or to weeds. —

If you desire to know, do not fear to ask. —

Study first to beautify thy face, but thy mind.

When you introduce a person pronounce the name distinctly and say whatever you can to make the introduction agreeable, such as an old and valued friend, a schoolfellow of mine, an old acquaintance of our family etc. —

Keep on good terms with your wife, your stomach and your conscience. —

Never stare about you in a room as if you were taking stock! —

An honest moral is better than a careless oath. —

Gold is the dust that blinds all eyes. —

Dirty windows speak to the passersby of the negligence of the inmates

Pages from the notebooks of Mrs. Robert Turner (of Shaw) b.1833.

Curzon St., Oldham. 31st August, 1885.

Advertisements, 1881.

The main time for celebration in the worker's year was Rushbearing Saturday which took place at the end of August each year. Records dating back to 1587 explain that rushes were strewn onto church floors for "coolness and pleasant smell" in summer, and for warmth in winter. However, the practice seems to have lost any religious significance as early as 1811, when we are told that "these days we find the rushcarts end anywhere but at the church".

"Oldham Wakes" has evolved from rushbearing, which was a religious ceremony. During the eve of rushbearing, through the night, the "Wakers", who were keeping awake to devote the night to prayer felt the need for suitable refreshment, so this annual "Wake" developed into an annual carousal, with amusement booths and ginger-bread stalls.

The number of rushcarts and the extent of celebrations depended entirely on how much money there was to spare. 1810 was a good year, with "nine rushcarts, high spending and much fighting", and 1818 is recorded as having "seven carts and one waggon . . . They were all superbly dect with silver plate and other rich emblems . . . and was an opportunity

8

for showing hospitality and indulging in beef, beer and other luxuries". However, only a short time later, "there was not one rushcart. Owing to these disturbed times, the lower class were for growing careful and using economy. They mostly brued there own beer . . . and the ale houses were very thinly attended".

Cotton spinning, coal mining and engineering went hand-in-hand during Oldham's industrial revolution. Demand for coal as fuel for a growing cotton industry meant that the number of mines increased, and the older ones were dug deeper. As the mines went deeper, flooding became a hazard, but with the availability of the steam engine for pumping, this was overcome, and by the 1830's coal production was an important source of employment.

The mechanisation of the textile industry saw the beginning of the engineering industry in the town. This evolved over a number of years, as skilled workers had to be brought from elsewhere, and new ones trained. Rollers for cotton machinery were being produced in 1816, and spinning mules were in demand. By 1830 Henry Platt was producing carding engines at Hartford Mill, Greenacres, and engineering was a growing industry.

Advertisement, 1878. ▼

Advertisement, 1918. ▼

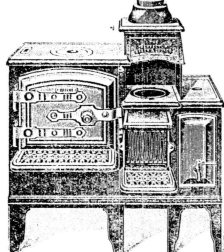

"PERFECTUM" COOKING STOVE

With Open & Close Fire. Registered No. 461,125

SIZES :   OVENS :
36in. wide.   15in. wide.
35in. high.   12in. high.
15in. back.   15in. back.

42in. wide.   16in. wide.
38in. high.   16in. high.
15in. back.   15in. back.

ALL KINDS OF KITCHEN RANGES.
COMBINATION GAS and COAL RANGES.
GAS STOVES and GAS BOILERS.
DRAWING and DINING ROOM MANTELS.
BARLESS FIRES.
INTERIOR GRATES and REGISTERS.
TILE CHEEKS.
TILE HEARTHS and TILE CURBS.
ELECTRO-PLATING (NICKEL and SILVER).
BRASS WORK RE-LACQUERED.
ANTIQUE BRONZING.

RAIN-WATER PIPES & CONNECTIONS

Prices upon application to

THE

Yew Tree Iron Works Co.
LTD.

HOLLINWOOD, OLDHAM

Advertisement c.1890 for domestic kitchen utensils.

From these simple beginnings, we can see the development of a town whose population was mostly working class. Their diet was mostly plain. Having enough to eat was the prime objective, rather than variety. However, as communications developed, a greater variety of foods from other parts of the country became available, and spices from abroad added flavour. Methods of cooking were simple. Open fires were later supplemented by coal-heated ovens and by the late 1800's many houses had a fireplace with an oven on one side and a water-container on the other, so that the fire would warm the room, heat the oven for cooking, and provide hot water. As a result, many of the traditional recipes have evolved by using the ingredients which were readily available and cooking them simply, by whatever means the household had.

As many women went to work, foods which could be left cooking gently either on top of the fire or (later) in the oven at the side were the ones most used. These also had the advantage that long slow cooking made the cheaper cuts of meat tender. As money was not available for expensive meats, it was these cuts which were mostly used.

"Free" food was used when it could be caught. Rabbits, hares, pigeons, rooks were taken for food, and may well have been the sole source of meat for some families.

OLDHAM FAMILIES

– CHAPTER TWO –

The Industrial Revolution brought wealth to some businessmen in the town. The Lees family is the best remembered, having been actively involved in the life of the town and responsible for many philanthropic gestures.

The branch of the family which lived at Werneth Park is probably most well known. The house was built by Eli Lees, who, in 1874 on the marriage of his son Charles Edward to Sarah Anne Buckley made over the house to them and went to live at Lancaster Gate in London. Charles Edward Lees was the nephew of Asa Lees, producer of textile machinery, and he was responsible for supervising the two mills which Eli Lees owned.

Charles Edward and Sarah Anne (later Dame Sarah) had two daughters, one of whom, Marjory, born in 1878 at Werneth Park, was later to play a part in public life, locally and nationally. Charles Edward died in 1894, and a few years later his wife Sarah became involved in local affairs. By 1910 she was Mayor of Oldham (only the second woman in England to receive the honour), and in 1917 she was awarded the D.B.E. by the King, for her philanthropic work, particularly in wartime, becoming Dame Sarah Lees.

Her daughter Marjory followed her mother's footsteps. She served on the town council for fifteen years, and was made a Freeman of the Borough in 1933. She had been actively involved in Women's Suffrage from 1910 on a national and international basis, as well as instituting and giving practical help to various causes in the town.

Dame Sarah died in 1934. Miss Marjory Lees gave Werneth Park to the town in 1936 and went to live in Windsor Road on the Coppice.

In contrast with most of the workpeople of the town, Dame Sarah and Miss Marjory Lees must

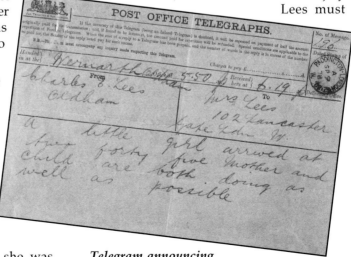

Telegram announcing the birth of Marjory Lees, 1878.

11

Menu cards—Lees family.

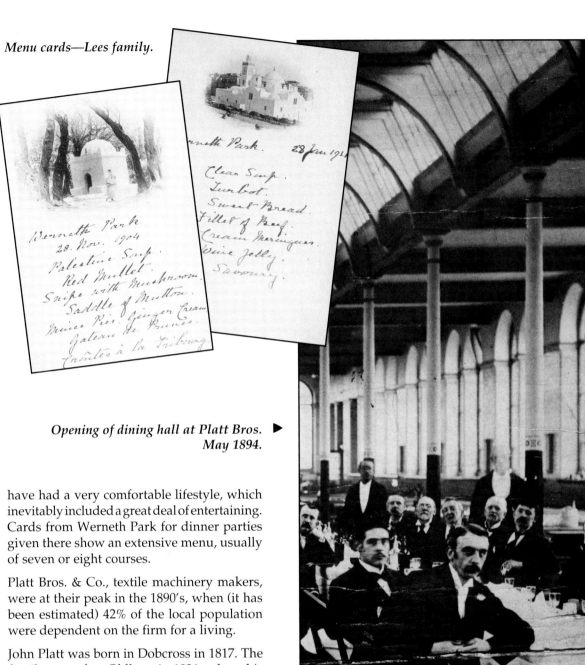

Wenneth Park
28. Nov. 1904
Palestine Soup.
Red Mullet.
Snipe with Mushroom.
Saddle of Mutton.
Mince Pies. Ginger Cream
Gâteau de Prunes.
Croûtes à la Fribourg.

...neth Park.   *28 Jan 195...*
Clear Soup.
Turbot.
Sweet-Bread.
Fillet of Beef.
Cream Meringues.
Wine Jelly.
Savoury.

Opening of dining hall at Platt Bros. ▶
May 1894.

have had a very comfortable lifestyle, which inevitably included a great deal of entertaining. Cards from Werneth Park for dinner parties given there show an extensive menu, usually of seven or eight courses.

Platt Bros. & Co., textile machinery makers, were at their peak in the 1890's, when (it has been estimated) 42% of the local population were dependent on the firm for a living.

John Platt was born in Dobcross in 1817. The family moved to Oldham in 1821, where his father, with Elijah Hibbert, laid the foundations of the business. John became senior partner in 1846, and under his dynamic management the firm was responsible for perfecting the carding machine, the roving frame and the self-acting mule.

The firm's expansion continued, whilst John Platt also played a part in the development of the town. He was three times Mayor of Oldham, and played a major role in the development of technical education and the promotion of new railways. From 1865 until his death in 1872 he represented the Borough in Parliament.

12

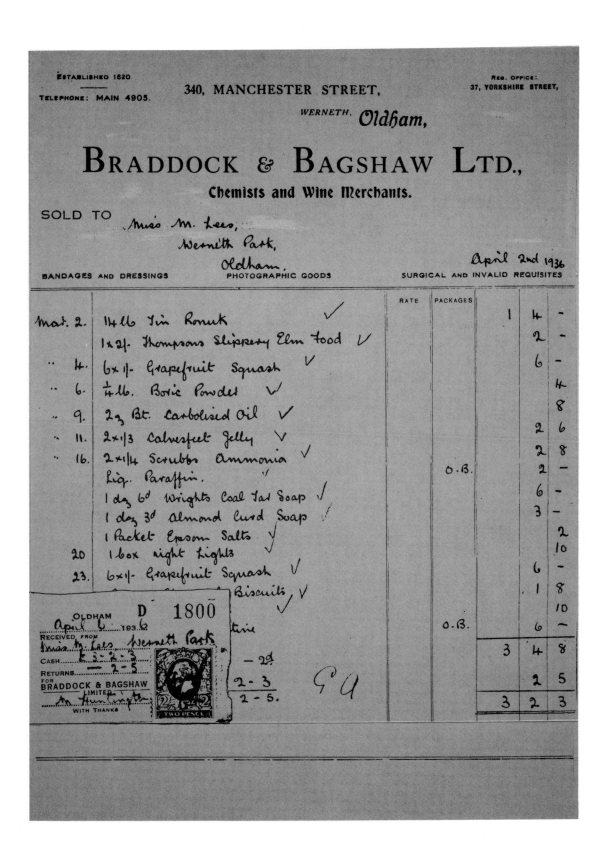

A bill from household accounts—Lees family, Werneth Park.

· CO-OPERATIVE MOVEMENT ·

– CHAPTER THREE –

The Co-operative movement, or "Co-op" is an established part of the life of many of the people of Oldham and surrounding areas. The Industrial Revolution had caused a great social change. People had moved from villages and small communities to areas where factories were being set up, which led to the growth of towns like Oldham. This, however, had the effect of leaving the worker, used to living in a close community, feeling uprooted, abandoned and unprotected. The need for mutual protection led to the formation of co-operatives. The Rochdale Pioneers, a group of twenty-eight artisans, mostly weavers, founded the Rochdale Equitable Pioneers in 1844, and the "Rochdale Principles" formed the foundation of the successful Co-operative movement.

Briefly, the four principles were:–

1. Open membership, without distinction of class or creed.
2. Democratic control (one member, one vote).
3. Limited interest on invested capital.
4. Elimination of profit *i.e.* distribution of all surplus in the form dividend on member's purchases.

In Oldham and the surrounding districts there had been early attempts at co-operative trading. As early as 1795 a group of working men and women, with a warehouse in Yorkshire Street, bought food and other

necessities as cheaply as possible, and sold them amongst themselves at a low price. Local traders were not pleased, and faced with violent opposition the group had to cease their operation after only a few years.

Other co-operative ventures included two at Failsworth, where around 1838 there was a joint effort to grow potatoes, and about ten years later there was the joint purchase of a cow by a number of young men. The cow was killed in a barn, and the meat sold to neighbours, but apparently they sold too cheaply or gave too much weight, as they did not make any profit.

The Co-operative movement as we know it in Oldham began in 1848, and prospered,

Tripe-dressing at James Dunkerley's, Oldham.

PICKLES AND SAUCES

MARMALADE AND PEELS

C.W.S. (MIDDLETON)
JAMS.

Dainty and *Delicious.*

ARE YOU DEAD

TO YOUR OWN INTERESTS?

THEN WHY PURCHASE

TEA, COFFEE,
OR **COCOA**

OTHER THAN THAT SUPPLIED BY

YOUR **WHOLESALE SOCIETY,**

ESTABLISHED BY

Your Capital for Your Benefit?

WAKE UP! TO YOUR POSITION AS A PART OWNER OF THE C.W.S. AND ITS DEPARTMENTS.

GENERAL HINTS TO TEACHERS OF COOKERY.

ISSUED BY THE GOVERNMENT BOARD OF EDUCATION.

1. In teaching cookery it is necessary, if the instruction given on the subject is to be of the highest *practical* value, that it shall be *definite*, *systematic*, and *progressive*.

2. Begin a series of lessons by teaching the children what cookery is, *i.e.*, the art of preparing food so that it becomes more *palatable* and *digestible* than in its raw condition. Let these two terms be explained in the simplest manner possible. Endeavour to make the children realise the *importance* of this study.

3. Then teach the children what are the six primary methods of cookery, and in what their differences consist, what meats should be roasted or baked, what boiled, what stewed, etc., and the *reasons*.

4. At each of the practice lessons at the commencement of a course let one recipe be illustrative of one of these primary operations, and be careful that each child is thoroughly instructed in the *principles*. — Arrange the recipes with *method*, so that the lessons shall be *progressive*.

5. Although good discipline should be maintained, care should be taken to make the lessons *interesting*, and the children should be encouraged to ask questions.

6. The lessons are expected to include instruction in the following subjects :—

    I. Boiling meat or fish.
        Stewing meat.
        Frying meat or fish.
        Baking meat or fish.
        Broiling meat or fish.
        Roasting meat (when it can be conveniently managed).
        The re-cooking of cold meat.

7. Bear in mind that economy of *time*, *labour*, and *fuel* are of as great importance to working people as economy of material. Cottage cooking should be *simplified* as much as possible.

8. To make the children exact, let them weigh the ingredients, but as they will not have scales and weights in their own homes let them also be taught to *measure* them with ordinary cups and table-spoons.

9. The dishes taught in the first series of ten lessons should always be those which the children can *easily* carry out in their own homes. In the second and third series some others may occasionally be introduced, but all should be economical.

10. Take care that the children learn not only how to *make* the dishes, but how to *cook* them. The teacher should leave the cooking to the children as much as possible, but at the same time exercise sufficient supervision to prevent them from spoiling the dishes.

11. It is better to arrange for the children to work in couples, and to prepare small dishes, than for a large number to work together in preparing one large one. The more a child actually does herself in the preparation of a dish the more she will remember.

12. Explain to the children as *simply as possible* the food value of the materials they use, and try and disabuse their minds of hurtful prejudices, such as that skim milk is only fit for pigs.

    In examining the elder girls it would be well to give them occasionally such questions as the following as exercises, allowing them time — say a week — to well think out the answers.

> 5. Although good discipline should be maintained, care should be taken to make the lessons *interesting*, and the children should be encouraged to ask questions.

> 8. To make the children exact, let them weigh the ingredients, but as they will not have scales and weights in their own homes let them also be taught to *measure* them with ordinary cups and table-spoons.

probably due to following the Rochdale Principles, the main one of which was that dividend was paid on members' purchases. There were two main societies, the Oldham Equitable and the Oldham Industrial Society, whose place of business was in Manchester Street (best remembered as King Street Stores). The Crompton Co-operative Provident Society was started in 1851, the Royton Industrial Co-operative Society was formed in 1857, and the Failsworth Industrial Society was founded in 1859 in a house in "Clem Guts Entry".

As we have seen, the ventures were successful due to the dividend being paid on purchases. It was a very simple system. Each member had a "check number". Every time a purchase was made, the amount was recorded. These amounts were added up, and every quarter a dividend, or "divi", would be paid to that check number. It could be saved in the share account, or drawn out immediately. It offered a convenient method of being thrifty without apparent sacrifice. Many people will remember buying their weekly groceries from the Co-op. Children sent to buy goods were always told "Remember the check number", and they had to come home with the small perforated "check" on which was written the check number and the amount spent. Not only groceries were eligible for dividend. All goods and services supplied by the Societies carried the benefit, even funerals.

Every quarter the dividend, or "divi" was paid. For many families the payment was like manna from heaven. No money had been "saved" as such, and yet because they had bought their groceries and household goods from the Co-op, they received a lump-sum payment. The amount varied from year to year, but was occasionally as much as 3/6d. in the pound (17½p dividend for every £1 spent).

During the Second World War, statistics show that one in four of all Britons were registered for food rations with a Co-op—about eleven million registrations. The Co-op's made their operations cover a wide range of social and educational efforts, almost pre-empting the work of the local authorities. People remember as children being able to have a new pair of shoes because the "divi" had been paid out. There were schemes advertised in some societies for free death benefit, which promised that "every purchase increased the death benefit". On a lighter note, the Failsworth Society around the 1930's and 1940's held a gala day at Brookdale Park in the summer for children, with organised sports and races, and "bun and milk" for a penny. The rock buns were plain, but large, the milk was fresh and the novelty of having a picnic in the park with the gala going on around was memorable for children whose usual playground was the street or the backyard.

Education was promoted through the movement, and a cookery book produced in the 1920's carried not only recipes but "General hints to teachers of cookery", issued by the Government Board of Education. One hint was to "make the lessons interesting, and the children should be encouraged to ask questions", which was quite a progressive educational attitude.

– CHAPTER FOUR –

OLDHAM EVENING CHRONICLE, MON. MAY 3, 1926

"NOT A GLEAM OF HOPE"

INDUSTRY IN PERIL

GENERAL STRIKE CERTAIN

Headlines from the "Oldham Chronicle", May 1st and May 3rd 1926.

The Great War, the "War to end all wars" began in 1914 and ended in 1918. The British population at first thought that it would be a short-lived affair—that it would be over in a matter of a few months. There was no doubt in their minds that the British would be the victors. The people of Oldham were no exception, but by June 1915, their buoyant mood was tempered by the news that many Oldham families had lost men at Gallipoli. By the end of 1915, 15,000 Oldham men had volunteered for active service and after conscription came into force in 1916 more were to follow.

The fact that men had to go to war meant that opportunities were opened for women to enter occupations previously restricted. Oldham traditionally had a large force of female employees in the textile industry, but other spheres of employment were now opened up. More women in employment meant more women out of the home environment, with the consequential changes in housekeeping.

Because of the war, there were problems with food supply. During 1917, enemy submarines were successfully attacking British merchant ships which were carrying food, with the object of starving the country into submission. Queuing for food was prevalent, and in Oldham a simple form of rationing was devised by the Oldham Food Control Committee; rent books or rate papers had to be produced in order to get a ration of tea, butter and other fats. Three National Soup Kitchens were opened in the town. Ingenuity and economy were necessary in this Great War, as in the later one, to keep families fed and healthy.

OLDHAM THROUGH THE YEARS
The COTTON FAMINE years
by ELGIN

BY THE END OF AUGUST, 1862, THE COTTON FAMINE WAS MAKING ITSELF FELT IN THE HOMES OF OLDHAM COTTON OPERATIVES.

SOUP KITCHEN!

THE NOW-VANISHED THEATRE ROYAL IN HORSEDGE ST. WAS OPENED AS A SOUP KITCHEN AND BRADDOCK'S ASSEMBLY ROOM ON THE IRON RAILINGS WAS RENTED BY THE LONDON RELIEF COMMITTEE FOR THE STORAGE AND DISTRIBUTION OF CAST-OFF GARMENTS.

After the Armistice, signed on 11th November 1918, the workers returned from the trenches. During the war, cotton production had been down because of the lack of labour and the shortage of raw materials—imports of raw cotton had not been first priority with merchant shippers. There was an enormous demand for cotton cloth, and in Oldham the "Mill Boom" began. Owning a cotton mill was seen as the way to amass great wealth, and businessmen paid enormous sums to buy Lancashire mills, envisaging continuing large profits. Unfortunately, they were wrong. The Lancashire mills had lost markets during the war to India and Japan, who had built their own mills equipped with the most modern machinery. They began to supply their own markets and some traditionally British ones. The cotton mills of Lancashire had had little modernisation or investment in machinery, and could not compete. As a result, by 1921, short-time working was in force, and the local newspaper reported that "unemployment and partial employment is general in Lancashire". By February 1921, 1,600 men were unemployed, and 19,000 on short-time (out of a total population of 145,000). The local authority devised schemes of street improvements in an attempt to find employment for some of the out-of-work men.

The "slump" continued. For over a decade the textile industry and the associated textile machinery industry in Oldham suffered, as did the workers and their families. During those years, for those workers food was simple and not plentiful. H. V. Morton, writing a newspaper column at the time describes as "... most typical of Lancashire? ... black puddings hanging ready for sale, windows full of tripe, like astrakhan—tripe that is good to eat cold with vinegar, so that it tastes like an iced bath sponge—hot-pot, potato cakes, brown and warm ...".

Christmas was a time for philanthropy. On Christmas morning the children of unemployed parents were given breakfast at the Equitable and Industrial Societies' halls, vouchers were sent to families in poor circumstances, and Christmas puddings were distributed.

Market Place, 1930's.
Wilkinson's butcher's, Glodwick.
Dunkerley's tripe dresser's, Manchester St.
Ramsden's pork butcher's, Yorkshire St.

Curzon St., Oldham, c.1910. Mr. Thomas Morris (standing left) won prizes for his window displays.

Advertisement from 1920.

Advertisements from 1926.

and between 1926 and 1935, the number of people in Oldham and district employed in the textile industry declined from about 51,800 to 29,800.

The Depression of 1929 which began with the Wall Street crash in America was another factor in this time of hardship. Unemployment grew worse and the national financial crisis in 1931, with the formation of a National Government, led to the institution of one of the most hated ways of providing benefit—the "Means Test". Application for benefit had to be made to the local Public Assistance Committee, and on proving destitution, benefit would be given. The system was embarrassing for those who had to administer it and humiliating for the applicants.

In Oldham the Public Assistance Committee at first refused to administer the Means Test, but pressure was brought to bear by the Ministry of Labour, who forced it upon them. Walter Greenwood, author of "Love on the Dole", visited Oldham in 1933 and wrote of what he saw:

"I recall the hectic days of a decade past when Oldham was a magnet for the whole of the country: golden days when profits were sky-rocketing: exciting days when Oldham public houses were transformed into miniature stock exchanges; days when London financiers

1926 was a disastrous year nationally. A dispute by miners, who refused to negotiate with their employers, saying "Not a penny off the pay, not a minute off the day", led to the General Strike, when the whole country was at a standstill. Slowly the workers returned, and in Lancashire there came the realisation that something had to be done to attempt to save the cotton industry for the future. At the end of the decade, the Lancashire Cotton Corporation was formed in an attempt to rationalise. This led to further unemployment,

W. Cockcroft Confectioners, Brook Street, Oldham.

▲ *Mr. Lambert, milkroundsman, outside Oldham Park gates, c.1900.*
▼ *Delivery cart used by Dunkerley's tripe dressers, c.1900.*

Advertisement for proprietary medicine, with a testimonial from Oldham.

journeyed to deal in shares with operatives come straight from spinning mill and weaving shed. Fabulous days when everybody was making a fortune. Ten years ago! . . .

I sought the man and woman in the street . . . Standing gazing in the corner shop's window was a typical Lancashire housewife. Small, pale-complexioned, straight dark hair neatly parted, clean white apron, grey shawl and clogs, she seemed to be weighing the pros and cons of what to buy . . .

We can't grumble. He keeps pretty reg'lar at work. Thurz them as is workin' and thurz them as ain't, same as other places. Me sister, her husband's bin out twelve months and mill where she works 's bin shut down. But Ah'm lucky wi' him bein' kep' on pretty reg'lar.

He tells me as thurz some fam'lies livin' on two meals a day, but that ain't nowt fresh. Why, when Ah first started at mill after me feyther died—he left me ma wi' eight—it tuk us all our time t' feed 'um on fried bread. O' course, my chap meks textile machinery an' they're busier there . . . But it don't do t' grumble, not when y' see some o' the fam'lies round here."

The mayor of the time, Alderman E. Bardsley, also spoke of the "wonderful spirit the people have shown in the face of adverse circumstances and bitter depression . . . an unfailing cheerfulness though women have constantly been struggling to make both ends meet and the men ever wondering what they could do to improve the conditions of the home".

Only in the latter half of the 1930's was there any sign of improvement in the town's prosperity. 1937 was the first year since the General Strike when trading in textiles was profitable, and there was a slight growth during the early months of 1939. But Oldham was to be caught up in national and international events. Once again, war clouds were on the horizon and, in anticipation of national defence needs, Ferranti planned to extend their engineering plant, and Platts gained a substantial war office contract.

The town was once again to reach virtually full employment when Britain went to war, on 3rd September 1939.

• HOMES 1920'S AND 1930'S •

– CHAPTER FIVE –

Conditions in the homes of Oldham during the first thirty or forty years of this century were very variable. There was the obvious social difference, where some families were wealthier than the rest, and were able to afford large houses and cook and eat extravagantly. Working class families had to be prudent in their spending on food, and "filling food" was the most desirable. Baking was done at home, and most women had a particular day of the week, usually towards the weekend, often on Saturday, which was "Baking Day". Loaves of bread would be baked, and as the oven became cool, pies and cakes would be put to cook more slowly. These pies and cakes would be eaten during the following week. Fresh bread could be bought at the baker's, but for most families "shop-bought" cakes and pies were an extravagance or simply unaffordable.

The kitchens of the time were a far cry from today's kitchens. Even into the 1930's it was not unusual in the many terraced houses in the town for the cooking still to be done in the oven next to the living room fire. However, more families were able to afford a cooker. The gas stove, with a very simple regulator to control the oven's temperature, was the most popular, as cooking by gas was cheaper than cooking by electricity and by 1925, 35,000 gas cookers were in use in the town. But electric appliances were becoming more widely available, and organisations such as the Electrical Association of Women, founded in 1925, (with a branch in Oldham) actively promoted the use of electricity. Dr. Ferranti, founder of the Ferranti company, which employed many workers at the Hollinwood factory, had an all-electric kitchen at his home, and during the 1930's this was the aim of middle-class ladies of the town. The cookers were very unsophisticated by present-day standards, and were made to last.

Garside Fold.

▲ *Factory Fold.*
Photograph taken 1936.

▼ *Rear of 10–16 Cemetery St.*
Photograph taken c.1935.

The gas and electricity industries were at this time not nationally owned. Gas had been manufactured in Oldham since 1823, with the Corporation taking responsibility for its production in 1853. Gas production was eventually centralised at Higginshaw Gas Works (which was updated and officially opened in 1933) supplemented by production at Hollinwood Gas Works.

Electricity was generated at Rhodes Bank Generating Station from 1894. Oldham Corporation was empowered to supply power for lighting, but not until 1926 was it allowed to sell electrical fittings or apparatus. By 1929, it was actively promoting the use of electricity in the home. Customers were encouraged to buy or hire cookers, and the special flat-bottomed pans to use on the cookers could also be hired. Between 1929 and 1937 more than 3,000 cookers had been supplied. In the 1930's, the refrigerator became the status symbol of middle-class homes, and added a new dimension to home cooking.

There were showrooms for both gas and electricity services where appliances could be bought and bills paid, though probably the majority of families paid for their gas or electricity by "penny in the slot" meters. The prudent housewife would make sure before starting her baking that the meter had a penny or two put into it so that the gas would not go out before the baking was finished.

Both the gas and the electricity industries were nationalised after the Second World War, thus moving out of the control of Oldham Corporation and other local authorities.

The variety of food eaten depended (as in earlier days) on what was available and what could be afforded. Most food was home-produced, which meant that the climate limited the variety, and seasonal foods were used to their best advantage. Surplus crops were bottled, preserved, jammed or jellied by provident housewives for use in the winter when fresh fruits and vegetables were not available.

The British Empire was great (though possibly not as great as it had been) and there was in existence the "Empire Marketing Board" in London, promoting the use of foods from the Commonwealth countries, and indirectly marketing the British Empire itself. Not

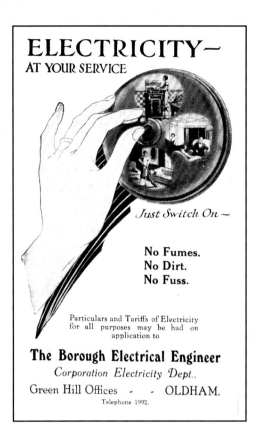

surprisingly it had the support of the King and he allowed his chef to give a recipe for "An Empire Christmas pudding".

However, even in 1928, the type of food available and eaten was not a great deal different from the available common foods of 1802. A list of the most commonly purchased foods in 1928 consists of:–

Herring	Sugar	Potatoes
Rabbit	Jam	Carrots
Bacon	Flour	English Onions
Beef	Oatmeal	Cauliflower
Mutton	Bread	Brussels Sprouts
Egg	Chocolate	Apples
Milk	Dripping	Butter

Some of the dishes produced from these foods were more sophisticated than those of 1802, but on the whole "plain cooking" was still the accepted norm for family meals. However, dietary deficiencies were being criticised. One magazine article of the time, considering the nation's diet noted that "insufficient fruit and vegetables, both fresh and cooked, are included; that animal flesh could often be substituted by cheese dishes, lentils, haricot particularly in the hand-written recipe books *e.g.* "put in enough sugar ...", but stated cooking temperatures reflect the fact that the ovens they were using were imprecise instruments. The coal oven's actual temperature depended upon the fire in the hearth next to it, and most gas ovens were regulated only as "High, Medium or Low". Electric cookers may have had a thermometer on the oven door, but it was difficult to control the oven temperature precisely. Instructions for cooking such as "The oven should not be too hot" and "Bake until it is done" appear in the National Mark recipe book of 1936, and the skill and judgement of the cook should not be discounted.

Familiar brand-names appear in the advertisements of the time. Heinz beans,

A Ferranti electric cooker c.1913. It cost £16.00.

beans, nuts and other forms of protein".

By the early 1930's the Government had devised the "National Mark", a trademark of controlled quality, marketed under the supervision and control of the Ministry of Agriculture and Fisheries. People were encouraged to buy National Mark beef, poultry, eggs, dairy products, flour, vegetables and preserved foods, and recipe books were available to encourage housewives to use seasonal foods.

Cakes and puddings (filling, inexpensive with a high carbohydrate content for instant energy) were popular at this time. They probably also helped to relieve a rather bland diet, and cookery books of the period have a large proportion of their recipes devoted to cake making. Instructions are often imprecise,

Enjoying a "savoury duck", or "duck-a-muffin".

The all-electric kitchen of Mr. Frank Rostron (of Ferranti Ltd.), 19 October 1930.

Ovaltine, Schweppes drinks, Grape-Nuts, Bisto and Stone's Ginger Wine may still be bought today, but many of the products advertised in the 20's and 30's have been lost in company mergers. What is notable in the advertising of the period is the popularity of laxative products and indigestion remedies, which were regularly but discreetly peddled. Presumably this says something about the diet of the time.

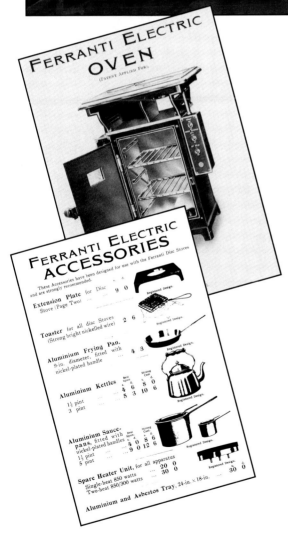

A 1937 display of an "Old Type Kitchen".

A "Modern Kitchen", 1937.

– CHAPTER SIX –

As everywhere else, the people of Oldham enjoyed getting together on social occasions. These varied, of course, according to one's place in the social strata, and the wedding reception of a mill owner's daughter would be quite different from that of a mill worker's daughter. Oldham Wakes was a popular time for weddings, when the town's industry closed down for a week, and the newly-weds could go off to the seaside (in the case of mill workers usually to Blackpool) for a short honeymoon. The wedding reception for working people was often at the bride's home to cut down on cost. Catering was done by the combined efforts of all the women in the family and would be as lavish as funds would allow.

Whit-Sunday Walks and Rose Queen celebrations 1930's.

The table would be covered with the best tablecloth, and set out on it there would be boiled ham and cold pressed tongue, salad of lettuce, tomatoes and hard-boiled eggs, boiled beetroot and pickled onions. Slices of bread, spread with "best butter" would accompany the cold meats and salad, and children would be made to eat at least one slice—"or you'll get nothing afterwards". What they would have missed would have been trifle. Every "occasion" had trifle, and for a wedding it would have been sherry trifle, with a glass or two of sweet sherry soaking into the cake at the bottom, and the whole finished off with cream and glacé cherries. Tinned fruit (peaches or pears) would be on offer, often served with evaporated milk poured over, as a cheap substitute for fresh cream. Red, yellow and orange jellies were inexpensive, and these were given to the children.

The wedding cake would have been home-made—no easy task with the imprecise ovens of the day, and many anxious moments would have been spent testing with a hatpin or darning needle to check that the middle of the cake was cooked, or peeping into the oven to

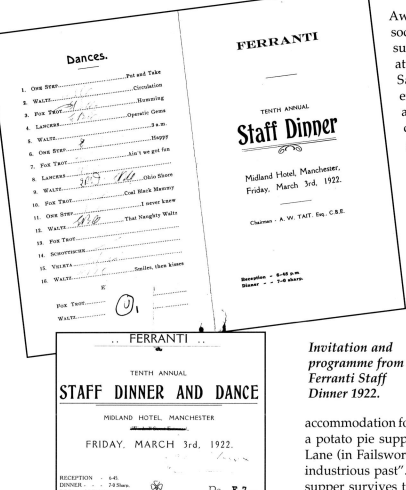

Dances.

1. One Step............Put and Take
2. Waltz............Circulation
3. Fox Trot............Humming
4. Lancers............Operatic Gems
   3 a.m.
5. Waltz............Happy
6. One Step............Ain't we got fun
7. Fox Trot............
8. Lancers............Ohio Shore
9. Waltz............Coal Black Mammy
10. Fox Trot............
11. One Step............I never knew
12. Waltz............That Naughty Waltz
13. Fox Trot............
14. Schottische............
15. Veleta............Smiles, then kisses
16. Waltz............

Fox Trot............
Waltz............

FERRANTI

—

TENTH ANNUAL

Staff Dinner

Midland Hotel, Manchester,
Friday, March 3rd, 1922.

—

Chairman - A. W. TAIT. Esq., C.B.E.

Reception - 6-45 p.m.
Dinner - 7-0 sharp.

.. FERRANTI ..

TENTH ANNUAL

STAFF DINNER AND DANCE

MIDLAND HOTEL, MANCHESTER

FRIDAY, MARCH 3rd, 1922.

RECEPTION - 6-45.
DINNER - 7-0 Sharp.
DRESS. OPTIONAL.   No. F.7.
Miss Smith.

Invitation and programme from Ferranti Staff Dinner 1922.

Away from home, a popular social event was a potato pie supper. This might take place at a church hall, usually on Saturday evening, with entertainment designed for all the family—usually dancing for the adults and games for the children. The potato pies, made in large brown dishes were served halfway through the evening, with everyone queuing for their plateful and helping themselves from the large bowls of pickled red cabbage which had been prepared as an accompaniment.

A newspaper article in the 1920's refers to "a loomhouse, denuded of its machinery . . . in recent days provided accommodation for a whist drive followed by a potato pie supper . . . Pole Lane and Back Lane (in Failsworth) have their relics of this industrious past". The traditional potato-pie supper survives today, usually as a form of fund-raising event, and is always popular.

Further up the social scale entertaining was often designed to impress the guests. A suggestion for a "light refreshments" for a dance at home includes eggs in aspic, sausage rolls, lobster cutlets, vol-au-vent of veal and bouchées à la Reine, followed by trifles, charlotte rousses, caramel creams, ginger creams and rum babas. Sandwiches, ice creams and home-made orangeade, lemonade, claret cup

A dance-card from 1921.

Hollinwood Institute
Byron Street
❖
Select Dance
In the above Hall
Saturday, Apr. 16th, 1921

Pianist—Mr. W. KINSMAN
An Efficient M.C. will be in attendance

❖

To commence at 7-0 p.m.
Programme - 1/9
(Including Refreshments)

ensure that the cake was not burning. Ever mindful of the cost of ingredients for a rich wedding cake, it <u>had</u> to be "just right".

The icing of the cake would also be done at home. It was usually very simply iced, as it would probably have to be done in fairly cramped conditions in the living-kitchen, with the other family activities going on all around. When finished, it would be set on a tall glass cakestand and have pride of place at the reception. As many guests as possible would be seated around the table in the living room (often referred to as "the house"). Children would if necessary be seated at a smaller table, or put into the kitchen to have their meal all together. Chairs and stools would be borrowed from neighbours for the occasion, and relatives would loan their best tea set and cutlery. It was quite genuinely a family affair, and the highest accolade was for it to be considered "a good do" by everyone who was invited.

and cider cup were also to be provided. The preparation of dishes for such a menu would have been very time consuming, but it was considered that catering for fifty guests was quite practical in a middle class home (with servants).

Some firms held a "staff dinner" for salaried staff. Ferranti started their tradition early in the 1900's, inviting their staff to the Midland Hotel in Manchester for a six-course dinner followed by a musical programme (which traditionally included the song "My Old Shako") and dancing. This was a highlight in the firm's year, and was one of the few opportunities some of the staff had to have dinner in such luxurious surroundings. Dr. Ferranti was a patriarchal figure, and the company had a reputation as "a family firm" and certainly paid competitive wages.

In 1932 skilled mechanics in the engineering industry earned 56 shillings (£2.80) per week for a 48-hour working week, but salaries in the engineering industry were never high enough to enable employees to dine at the Midland Hotel unless someone else was footing the bill.

"Albion St., Oldham". John Stanley Bates. Dated 1911.

▲ *Typical Edwardian tea-table.*

▲ *Typical 1930's tea-table.*

▼ *Tea loaf (see p.59).*

WARTIME • 1939–1945 •

– CHAPTER SEVEN –

The outbreak of World War Two on 3rd September 1939, was to alter the face of Oldham, maybe not as directly as some towns which suffered more severe bombing, but by the change in emphasis of employment. Many men joined the forces and went away from home, whilst local factories were deployed in war work. Ferranti were turning out munitions, and A.V. Roe's were building bombers. Women were recruited to areas of employment not traditionally associated with female labour. The cotton mills had always employed large numbers of women, but engineering had been principally a masculine province.

Women who had never worked outside the home at all were recruited for this war work, whilst others who had been employed in domestic service eventually found war work a more congenial and lucrative way to make a living.

On "the Home Front", everyone was reminded that the war effort was a communal one. "Make do and Mend", "Dig for Victory", "Save Fuel for the Factories" were campaigns with a very necessary practical motive behind them, heightening public awareness by their catchy slogans, constantly repeated.

As early as July 1939, the Government was issuing public information leaflets describing contingency plans in the event of war, when the Government would take over responsibility for obtaining and distributing main food supplies. A Ministry of Food was to be set up, with local distribution in the hands of a local Food Control Committee. In Oldham, Mr. T. Alker, the Town Clerk was the local Food Controller, with a committee of fifteen people. Five had to be retail traders and ten were to represent "consumers of all classes". Two of the consumers were to be women.

© Crown Copyright 1989.

One of the leaflets gives the basic outline of the rationing scheme which was followed during (and after) the war.

Rationing was the way of ensuring that everyone would have their fair share in the likely event of food shortages. As early as October 1939, retailers were obliged to register with their local Food Control Committee in order to receive licenses to sell a very wide variety of foods. Bacon, biscuits, bread, breakfast cereals, butter, cakes, cheese, chocolate and sugar confectionery, coffee, cocoa, compound lard, cream, edible or cooking fats, eggs, fish, flour, fruit, ham, honey, jam, lard, margarine, meat, milk, potatoes, poultry, game and rabbits, rice, sausages, sugar, syrup, tea, vegetables were all regulated foods.

Ration books were issued to everyone in 1939, although rationing was not implemented until 8th January 1940. Before the implementation, the temptation was to stockpile, in spite of exhortations by the authorities that this was anti-social. Poorer families were particularly affected, as they could not afford to hoard, and had to live with the consequent shortages. When rationing was introduced, it did have the effect of ensuring that everyone who could afford it was able to have their entire food ration.

The weekly amount of various commodities was dependent upon supplies. Initially, rations were generous, but as the war progressed quantities were reduced and some goods disappeared from the shops entirely. As the merchant shipping fleet came under attack, many ships carrying foods from abroad were sunk, cargoes were lost, and the vessels could not be replaced, leaving Britain to face food shortages.

However, due to rationing everyone received a minimum amount of food, and poorer families probably ate a far better-balanced diet during the war than at any time before.

During 1942, the weekly ration of standard foods was 3 ounces of cheese, 2 ounces of butter, 6 ounces of cooking fat and margarine and 4 ounces of bacon.

The emphasis in cooking was to provide interesting meals with available ingredients. The cooks were often housewives doing war work, so time-saving had to be considered.

Information issued in 1939.

© *Crown Copyright 1989.*

ISSUED BY THE MF MINISTRY OF FOOD

HOW TO GET YOUR NEW RATION BOOKS

CUT THIS OUT FOR REFERENCE

1. See that the particulars on your identity card and food ration books (both buff and green) are correct, and that they *agree*. If these are not exactly the same, *do not alter them yourself*, but take both to your Food Office immediately.

2. Fill in page 3 of your present ration book (the Reference Leaf) including Section Z. But do not cut out this page.

GENERAL (Buff) BOOK

CHILD'S (Green) BOOK

3. On page 4 of the General (buff) Book (the back of the Reference Leaf), write the name and address of your present Milk retailer. On page 4 of the Child's (green) Book, write the names and addresses of the child's present Milk, Meat, and Eggs retailers. Never mind the printing; write on top of it. *Do not take out the page.*

4. Make sure that page 38 of your present ration book has been properly filled in.

5. Look out for A.B.C. posters like this in local cinemas, post offices, food offices, etc., and for advertisements in your local papers. Opposite your initial you will see where you should call and when. *The office will be situated in your own food control area.* It's no use going to any other place, or at any other time, than that shown on the poster or advertisements.

The new books and cards will be prepared and issued in alphabetical order of surnames. If there are different surnames in your household, it will mean more than one visit, but less waiting when you get there.

A friend can go for you, but *only* at the time, and place advertised for *your* surname.

6. Take your identity card and present ration book when you go for your new ones. You need not take personal points or clothing book. You will be given your new food ration book with personal points and clothing book (bound together but detachable) and, if you are over 16, a new identity card.

"under the counter") were served without comment. Families tucked into "meat puddings" blissfully unaware that the steak filling was actually horsemeat.

Butter and margarine rations at times were very low, and the fatless sponge cake was part of every Oldham housewife's baking repertoire. Cakes were for Sundays or special occasions, and meagre rations were carefully saved and shared if any family was having a celebration—perhaps a son coming home on leave, or a wedding in the family.

Shopping for "the rations" was a weekly event. All customers had to be registered with a retailer. Pre-packaging was unusual, and foods such as sugar, butter, tea, cheese were weighed and packed when purchased. A judicious eye was kept on the scales as the goods were weighed out, and any shopkeeper attempting to give "short rations" would be firmly reminded of the current allowance. When the goods were gathered together, the ration books would be handed over and the retailer had to cut out coupons relating to that particular week. The ration book became something of a symbol of Britain at war. Housewives always ensured that the ration books were in "a safe place", and the book itself carried the warning "in the event of your being compelled to leave home because of air raids . . . take this book with you".

Oldham supported the "Dig for Victory" effort by turning the parks into allotments. Land

Ration book issued 1939, showing page of "coupons".

© Crown Copyright 1989.

Substitutes such as dried egg and dried milk had to be incorporated into recipes when the fresh foods were not available. Great ingenuity was shown in combining foods, and ways of serving non-rationed meats were devised. Offal was not rationed, nor was horsemeat, and these, when available, (sometimes from

WARTIME CODE FOR SHOPPERS

A WARTIME code of conduct for shoppers has been drawn up by Mr. Dennis Morgan, secretary of the Cardiff Chamber of Trade. The six points are:–

1. When confronted by increased charges do not immediately assume profiteering. Give the shopkeeper's a chance to justify the increase. Keep your eye on controlled prices.
2. Order well in advance. Place orders by the week.
3. Shop early.
4. Carry home your purchases and so save petrol for delivery vans.
5. Pay cash or pay weekly.
6. Be patient with shop assistants. They are working under difficulties.

THIS IS A TRUE STORY

"Graf Spee" mother in action

1. Widowed Mrs. Stephens' son was on the Ajax. How excitedly she heard of the River Plate battle!

2. But back at her job as a furrier she began to think : "He's fighting ; why shouldn't *I* ?"

3. So she asked at the Employment Exchange if they could find her a war-winning job.

4. Here she is at a Government Training Centre, learning about Munitions.

5. The work is interesting, the pay is good, the food and companionship are grand.

6. And when her son gets le[...] again, won't he be proud of [...] fighting mother !

Every woman with a husband, son or sweetheart in t[...] Forces can do like Mrs. Stephens, and help them in the battl[...] Ask your Local Office of the Ministry of Labour an[...] National Service how *YOU* can learn real War Work[...]

YOUR DUTY NOW IS WAR WORK

War Work True Story No. 8. Founded on facts, but names are fictitious

---

"Among those present.."

KALE was among the vegetables on your Greengrocer's counter last season. But you never know if it is going to put in an appearance *this* winter. That's where "Victory Diggers" score—they grow their own, and make *sure* of supplies. Take a leaf out of their book and start Digging for Victory NOW. If you haven't a garden, get an allotment, and be sure of vegetables for your family all the year round. An hour in the garden saves one in a queue.

DIG FOR VICTORY NOW!

★★★ If you haven't a garden, ask your Local Council for an allotment. Send NOW for Free pictorial leaflets "HOW TO DIG" and "HOW TO CROP" to Ministry of Agriculture, Dept. D103, Hotel Lindum, St. Annes-on-Sea, Lancs.

ISSUED BY THE MINISTRY OF AGRICULTURE

During the War, the Government used advertisements to encourage patriotism.

FOOD IS A MUNITION OF WAR

DON'T WASTE IT

Rally round the Flag when you gather round the table

which was used for playing games was exempt, but other land was let out to individuals to grow their own vegetables, although the use of the land for grazing was prohibited. Copster Park had 120 allotments.

Hens were kept in many Oldham backyards and back gardens, and henfood was available, although coupons equivalent to an egg ration had to be given up for it.

British-grown if not home-grown vegetables were recognised as a cheap, available source of nutrition, and the Ministry of Food devised "Doctor Carrot" and "Carroty George" cartoon characters as a means of promoting vegetable consumption.

© Crown Copyright 1989.

Oldham was very fortunate in escaping the severe bombing attacks endured by many other towns. However, it did not escape completely; the town was hit several times in 1941. Reporting of incidents as they happened was not allowed, as there was a blackout on any news reporting which might assist the enemy.

By the end of 1944, when the war was five years old and there was hope that it might be ending, it was felt that some information could be revealed. The "Oldham Chronicle" for 7th November 1944 analysed the bomb damage which the town had suffered until then, so a clearer picture emerged.

It was towards the end of the war, when ironically Civil Defence regulations had been relaxed, that a V-bomb

Carroty George

© Crown Copyright 1989.

("flying bomb") attack took place at 5.30 in the morning of Christmas Eve, 1944. It was thought that the bomb had directed at Manchester and went off course. It landed on Abbeyhills, totally destroying several houses with consequent loss of life. The "Oldham Chronicle" reported that "not withstanding that Civil Defence and other personnel had not been standing by at posts and depots for some time there was an excellent response. Wardens and police were quickly on the scene, followed shortly afterwards by ambulances, rescue and casualty services. The Home Guard rescue squads also reported and gave good help. Valuable aid was rendered, too, by the National Fire Service. Mobile canteens and emergency feeding services were quickly at work".

VICTORY

VE-Day celebrations began on 8th May 1945, with the final capitulation of Germany. All over the country street parties were instantly organised. This longed-for day was celebrated

---

Bombs Damaged 3,410 Oldham Houses

"ALERT" HEARD 319 TIMES
Controller's Record of Raids

It can now be revealed that enemy action has damaged 3,410 houses in Oldham since June, 1940. Those totally destroyed numbered 28, seriously damaged and requiring demolition 29, extensively damaged 397, seriously damaged 1,417, and slightly damaged 1,539.

There have been 319 alerts, the last one on August 18, 1913. The longest alert was on December 22, 1940, when it lasted eleven hours, 48 minutes. From midnight on October 20 to midnight on October 21, 1940, there were seven alerts.

▲ *Hanging Hitler.*
Ferranti Ltd. Moston factory
victory celebrations, 1945.

Ferranti Ltd. Hollinwood ▼
works decorated for victory
celebrations, 1945.

by housewives bringing out into the streets all the food that could be spared to be pooled in a communal street celebration. VE-Day and the following day were announced as paid holidays for cotton and engineering employees amongst others, so everyone could join in the celebrations.

Bunting was strung from lampposts across the street, home-made posters bearing the words "VE Day" were stuck on front walls and gates, and everyone with a Union Jack hung it from the window. Dining tables and chairs were carried into the street and arranged in a long line, and as a mark of occasion "best" tablecloths were produced to spread on the tables.

The food was not lavish—lavish food was not available, but jam and potted meat sandwiches, jellies, sponge cakes and scones were the types of food which would have been found. The atmosphere at these parties was one of relief and hope. The War in Europe was over and the war with Japan was drawing to a close. Behind the gaiety and the laughter of 8th May lay six years of hard work, anxiety and sorrow. Everyone drank a toast on VE-Day to "Victory", and a hopeful future.

Street party to celebrate the end of World War 2, 1945.
St. George's Square, Chadderton. ▼

40

Cranberry Street, Glodwick.

– CHAPTER EIGHT –

Oldham has developed from a village to a town with a population of over 200,000. The indigenous population has been joined by people from other cultures, almost invariably here initially for one reason—the search for work.

From 1714 to 1832 the population of the town grew from 1,732 to 32,000. The development of the transport system brought men to be "navvies"—to cut the canals and make the roads which were to be so important to the Industrial Revolution. Hard on their heels came men to work in the newly sprung-up factories. Initially, these men came from Ireland and Scotland, from agricultural communities where life was hard and the prospect of earning a regular, relatively good wage in the cotton mills was enticing.

This pattern continued through the late nineteenth and early twentieth century. Men, followed by their families, would gravitate from the parts of Britain which had no work to wherever work could be found. The Potato Famine of 1846 caused a great exodus from Ireland and Scotland.

After the Second World War, in 1945, the town's industry was booming. There were jobs to spare in engineering, cotton spinning and coal-mining. British industry was on the move and Oldham had its part to play.

Manpower was needed—generally to fill unskilled or labouring jobs, and to fill this need came people from other communities. Polish ex-servicemen and refugees, White-Russian Ukrainian refugees, both men and women. They constituted an unskilled, but diligent labour force, in spite of the fact that many had suffered severe privations during the years of World War 2, which subsequently affected their health.

The West Indies (part of the Colonies until the 1950's) also provided labour. The majority of West Indians in Oldham came from Jamaica, an island which had traditionally grown sugar cane. However, failures in the crops led to unemployment, and the islanders looked to Britain to find work. By tradition a high proportion of West Indian women work, and Britain took advantage of this, employing them in hospitals as nurses and auxiliary workers.

The bulk of the Caribbean immigration came in the latter half of the 1950's, and was closely followed by immigrants from the Indian sub-continent, around 1960. The background for their arrival is that during the early 1950's the cotton industry in Lancashire was in a state of decline. The mills were running with outdated machinery, producing highly-priced goods which could not compete with cheap imports from the Third World. In 1959 the Cotton

42

Industry Act was passed. This encouraged mills to install new machinery, but because of its high cost it had to be run 24 hours a day, usually on three 8-hour shifts. The night-shift, because of its unsocial hours, without enhanced pay, was not attractive to local workers, but employers found that Bengali and Pakistani immigrants were prepared to work the night shifts and accept relatively low pay. These immigrants were generally men, who came alone to establish a home and were later joined by their families.

Indian families, originally from the state of Gujurat, have come to Oldham, often as refugees from East Africa, where they had earned their living as merchants. When the colonies became independent in the 1950's and 1960's the Asians were offered a choice: retain British citizenship or take up local citizenship. Many of the Asians had worked with the British in colonial days, and had a certain prestige. Consequently, many chose to retain their British citizenship. But the new African governments, not unnaturally, were running their countries in a new way, and the British Asian population found themselves without the power they had once held, without any position in society, and without jobs. So from Kenya, Uganda, Malawi and Tanzania they came to Britain, as refugees.

The other culture which has come to the town is from further East. Starting sometime during the 1950's, and continuing now, Hong Kong Chinese have come to Britain. They are mostly employed in the food industry, many owning or working in restaurants, fish and chip shops, take-away food shops or delicatessens. Generally they have not been involved in the manufacturing industries.

All these cultures—Ukrainian, Polish, Indian, Pakistani, Bangladeshi, West Indian and Chinese—have added another dimension to the social fabric of the town. Their religions and cultural traditions now form part of Oldham's everyday way of life.

Part of the cultural tradition is food, and we have absorbed almost without noticing the influences of those cultures. Oldham families as a normal part of their diet regularly enjoy what only forty years ago would have been regarded suspiciously as "foreign food". Curries, sweet and sour beef, filled dumplings and chilli dishes are becoming fairly commonplace. Food has been a way of crossing boundaries, and social integration has been helped along by members of different cultures meeting to share food and ideas.

UKRAINIAN FOOD

The customs and recipes associated with the religious festivals are still important. The Catholic and Orthodox churches are working together to keep the Ukrainian community flourishing, and in Oldham there is a strong community spirit. Lent, Easter and Christmas are the most important festivals. Special recipes are cooked and particular traditions are upheld in every household. As with the traditional food of Oldham, Ukrainian recipes are based upon what food was available in their homeland. Pork, lamb and poultry were the most common meats, cows being kept mainly for milk to drink and for cheese and butter production.

Cabbage, potatoes and beetroot were abundant and easily stored during the harsh winters. Grain (rye, wheat, barley and millet) was plentiful, and a great tradition of breadmaking grew up, with loaves long or round, soft or crusty, sometimes coated with poppy seeds. Buckwheat was also popular, used in savoury

The paska (Easter bread), ham, sausage, cheese, butter, krasa[...] ready to be taken to church on Easter morning for [...]

and sweet dishes. Puddings as we know them are not traditional, although sweetened buckwheat and pies are made. Fruit and cheese are more usually served at the end of a meal. Spices (apart from pepper) are not usual, and the most common flavourings are garlic and dill-weed.

The Easter feast really starts during Lent. Traditionally fat, butter, cheese, eggs, meat, buckwheat and salt were given up, and a simple diet followed. On Easter Sunday the family would gather together for a traditional Easter breakfast, when all the foods forbidden during the forty days of Lent would be included.

Christmas is celebrated according to the Julian calendar (in which Christmas Eve falls on 6th January). The supper of Christmas Eve is the culmination of a six-week Advent fast, and consists of twelve traditional dishes (signifying twelve apostles). The dishes are made with simple basic ingredients—wheat, barley, honey, beets, potatoes etc., but without any dairy produce, eggs or meat.

PAKISTANI AND BANGLADESHI FOOD

Family life and the maintenance of traditional roles are very important. The people are mainly Muslims, followers of the religion Islam, with strict dietary laws, including fasting between sunrise and sunset in the month of Ramadan. Muslim religion insists that meat must be halal meat (killed with a single stroke and with a prayer). Pork products are forbidden, as is alcohol.

The ingredients used in their recipes may be found widely throughout the town, in specialist shops, supermarkets or market stalls. The spices used in curries may be bought ready mixed or may be ground and mixed according to taste, and curries are made of beef, chicken, lamb or vegetables usually served with rice or flour preparations such as nan bread. Dishes of pulses (lentils and peas) are popular, and chapattis (flat pancakes) are a staple part of the diet. Curries are accompanied by a variety of side dishes such as chutney, pickles or yoghurt.

INDIAN FOOD

The religion of almost all Gujaratis is Hindu, and the orthodox Hindu is totally vegetarian. There are Hindus who are not totally orthodox, and for them meat-eating is allowed, although Hindus never eat the meat of the cow, which is the Hindu's sacred animal. Orthodox Hindus will not drink alcohol.

In a vegetarian diet special attention has to be paid to protein-rich foods, and peas, beans, lentils and nuts are important ingredients in Indian cookery. Pakoras or bhajias, the deep-fried vegetable fritters are an everyday sight on the delicatessen counter at the local supermarkets.

The religious festivals of Eid (Muslim) and Divali (Hindu) are celebrated in local schools, in the same way as Christmas. Children and parents bring food which has been prepared at home into school, the children wear their "special-occasion" clothes and the food is shared.

44

• UP TO THE MOMENT •

– CHAPTER NINE –

Just as the influence of other cultures and the growth of vegetarianism and "whole-food" eating as a concept has given another dimension to the food of Oldham since the Second World War, so has the "technological revolution". During the last war and in the 1950's, developments in technology and materials accelerated. Britain invested money in scientific and technological research, pioneering much of the world's innovative technological development. However, the computer, the transistor and the microchip were not part of everyday life until the 1960's and 1970's, when manufacturers were able to capitalise on the capabilities of electronics. Locally, the Ferranti electronics factory was in production, and playing its part in the new industrial revolution.

As a spin-off from industrial development, domestic applications of computers and microchips became more commonplace, and the past thirty years have seen an enormous change in the tasks imposed by housework and food preparation. In relation to earnings, the cost of electrical appliances has decreased and now the majority of Oldham homes have a cooker, electric kettle, pressure cooker, refrigerator, freezer, and many have a microwave oven.

A change in domestic lifestyle has also come about. Various theories have been propounded—the influence of television, the amount of time spent on television viewing, the absence of a designated dining area in many homes—but for whatever reason, many families do not eat their main meal together. The heart of the home is not now in the kitchen or round the table, and the types of food eaten and the methods of cooking them have changed.

Most present-day cooks, with the facility of an easy-to-clean, time-controlled cooker and a microwave oven will have no regrets at not having to light a fire in order to boil a kettle or cook food in the oven. No tears will be shed by not having to "blacklead" a grate to keep it looking clean, or clearing out the ashes from the fire. But there may be a pang of nostalgia from those who remember the times when having a family meal at home was more than just the consumption of food, however tasty. When a shared simple meal brought the family, often three generations, all together, in a small celebration of their heritage.

RECIPES WITH AN OLDHAM FLAVOUR

• SAVOURY DISHES •

Bacon Hot Pot
Beef Mould
Brawn
Cabbage and Apple
Carrots & Turnips
Celery Soup
Sour-Milk Cheese
Cheese and Onion Pie
Cheese, Egg & Milk
Cornish Pasties
Cow-heel Broth
Cow-heel and Beef
Ham and Bacon
Hash
Haslet
Hot Pot
Lentil Soup
Liver and Bacon
Meat (Rag) Puddings
Meat & Potato Pie
Mint Sauce (Fresh)
Mint Sauce (Preserved)
Mock Duck
Pea Soup
Potato Cakes (Fried)
Potato Cakes (Baked)
Potato Pie
Potted Ham
Potted Beef
Pressed Beef
Rabbit Casserole
Salmon Paste
'Duck' Hash
Savoury Ducks
Scotch Broth
Sheep's Head, Boiled
Shin of Beef Casserole
Steak and Onions
Ox Tongue

• UNRATIONED MEAT DISHES •

Tripe and Onions
Woolton Pie

• PUDDINGS & CAKES •

Bible Cake
Bread and Butter Pudding
Caramel Cornflake Crunch
Christmas Pudding
Coconut Crunch
Curd Cheese Cakes
Custard Pie
Dripping Cake
Dumplings
Eggless Cake
Flat-Cake (or Fatty Cake)
Fruit Cake (Rich)
Fruit Cake ("Everyday")
Fruit Crumble
Fruit Scones
Ginger Biscuits
Gingerbread
Ginger Crunch
Girdle Cakes
Liquidiser Almond Cake
Lancashire Nuts
Madeira Cake
Malt Loaf
Mincemeat
Orange Cake
Parkin
Granny's Parkin
Queen of Puddings
Rice Pudding
Rock Cakes
Roly Poly Pudding
Russian Sandwich
Shortbread

Syrup Tart
Treacle Layer Pudding
Trifle
Wholemeal Biscuits

• MISCELLANEOUS •
(Preserves & Drinks)

Bramble Jelly
Blackcurrant Jam (Microwave)
Marmalade
Quick Orange Marmalade
Lemon Curd
Chutney
Barley Water
Elderflower Champagne
Ginger Wine
Lemonade

• UKRAINIAN DISHES •

Khrusty (Dainties)
Borsch (Beetroot soup)
Kholodets (Jellied pigs feet)
Varenyky (Filled dumplings)
Cheese and Potato Filling (For Varenyky)
Holubtsi (Cabbage rolls)
Meat and Rice Filling (For Holubtsi)
Kurochky

• ASIAN RECIPES •

Aubergine Curry
Chapatis
Fried Onion
Lentil Curry
Meat Curry
Onion and Spinach Pakoras
Spicy Chicken Liver
Sweet Almond Pudding
Sweet Carrot Halva

Temperatures are in °Fahrenheit.

• SAVOURY DISHES •

• BACON HOT POT •

Place a layer of sliced potatoes in an oven dish. Sprinkle with chopped onion, dried sage, salt and pepper.

Repeat until dish is full. Put nobs of bacon fat or margarine and rashers of fat bacon on top. Cover with greaseproof paper and cook in moderate oven about $2\frac{1}{2}$ hours.

• BEEF MOULD •

1 lb. shin of beef	A few peppercorns
Seasoning	Water
2 cloves	

An excellent mould which is not merely a wartime expedient though it makes the most of meat ration. Wash beef, simmer gently in covered pan with water just to cover, adding cloves and peppercorns. When gristle is tender, remove. Cut meat into small pieces, return to pan. Simmer again without lid until liquid is sufficient only to prevent burning, stirring occasionally. Season, turn into basin or mould, leave to set overnight.

• BRAWN •

Ingredients:

1lb. fresh beef pieces	Pepper and salt
1 small cow-heel	2 quarts of water
A sprig of parsley	

Method: Put the beef pieces and the cow-heel into a saucepan, with the parsley, a little pepper and salt, and the cold water. Bring to the boil, remove any scum that rises, and then simmer for about 6 hours, until the meat will come away from the bones of the cow-heel, and the beef is tender. Turn all into a basin, take out the parsley, and remove the bones and cut the meat up small and turn the brawn mixture into a wetted mould. Cover with a plate with a weight on the top, and when cold turn out.

• CABBAGE AND APPLE •

1 lb. cabbage or red cabbage
1 or 2 apples
1 onion or 2 shallots
Salt to taste
Margarine or dripping
1 teacupful boiling water

Remove thick stalks of cabbage and shred as for salad. Peel, core and slice apples thinly, fry thinly sliced onion or shallots in fat. Add apple to pan and when yellow add cabbage. Stir well, add boiling water, cover with lid and cook 25 minutes, or till tender; serve very hot.

• CARROTS & TURNIPS •

Homely North Country way of mashing equal parts of boiled carrots and turnips together with a little fat and pepper should not be forgotten.

• CELERY SOUP •

1 Medium-sized head of celery
weighing about 1 lb.
1 onion
$1\frac{3}{4}$ pts. stock or water
$\frac{1}{4}$ pt. milk
1 oz. margarine
1 oz. flour
Pepper and salt

Method: Prepare the celery and the onion and cut into thin slices. Melt the fat in a pan, put in the vegetables and sauté with saucepan lid on, for 10–15 minutes, stirring or shaking pan to prevent burning. Add the stock and seasoning, and simmer gently until the vegetables are tender, 1–$1\frac{1}{2}$ hours. Rub through a hair sieve. Add the flour blended with the milk and boil 3–4 minutes. If liked, add 2 or 3 tablespoonfuls of cream. Serve with croûtons of fried bread.

• SOUR-MILK CHEESE •

The next time you have some sour milk turn it into sour-milk cheese. As soon as the milk has turned sour put it into a warm place and leave it until it is thick.

Than add about half a teaspoonful of salt to a pint of milk, stir well, put in a piece of muslin and tie up loosely.

Hang up to drain till the next day.

When drained, tighten the muslin, and press between two plates for an hour. It is then ready for the table.

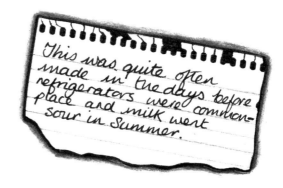

This was quite often made in the days before refrigerators were common-place and milk went sour in Summer.

• CHEESE AND ONION PIE •

Shortcrust pastry made with:

8 oz. S.R. flour	Pinch salt
4 oz. lard/margarine	Water to mix

Chop 1 large onion, and simmer gently in a little water for 10 minutes, until well softened.

Grease an 8" pie plate (an enamel or metal one is best, as it conducts the heat and the base of the pie is thoroughly cooked, but a pottery or Pyrex one can be used).

Roll out half the pastry and use it to line the pie plate.

Drain the onions and spread on the pastry. Chop 12 oz. cheese (Lancashire, Cheshire, Cheddar, Wensleydale are all good) and scatter over the onions. Season with salt and pepper.

Roll out the other half of the pastry. Moisten the edges of the base of the pie with milk. Put on the pastry topping, and trim the edges. Make slits in the top crust to allow steam to escape.

Brush with milk or beaten egg (to give a brown appearance when cooked) and bake at 325° for about 30 mins.

• CHEESE, EGG & MILK •

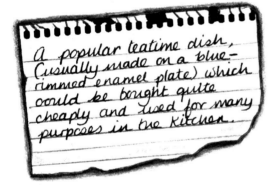

A popular teatime dish, (usually made on a blue-rimmed enamel plate) which could be bought quite cheaply and used for many purposes in the kitchen.

The housewife would prepare 1 plate for each person and put as many plates as possible into the oven together. A large family might have 2 "sittings", as all the plates would not fit in at once. When cooked, it would go straight to the table and be eaten with crusty bread.

For 1 person:–

Butter an enamel plate.

Chop, coarsely grate or crumble 4 oz. cheese onto the plate, according to the type used (Lancashire, Cheshire or Wensleydale are best, and Cheddar, though less crumbly, can be used).

Pour ¾ cup of milk over the cheese, dot with butter and place in a medium oven, (about 325°).

When the milk is hot and the cheese is melting, break an egg into the middle. Season with pepper and a little salt and put back into the oven until the egg is cooked. Serve immediately, with fresh bread.

• MEAT DISHES •

• CORNISH PASTIES •

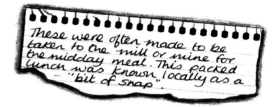

These were often made to be taken to the mill or mine for the midday meal. This packed lunch was known locally as a "bit of snap".

½ lb. Short Crust Pastry

Filling:
¼ lb. raw meat
2 tablespoonfuls potatoes
1 tablespoonful chopped onion
1 tablespoonful diced turnip
1 tablespoonful water
Pepper, salt

Method: Cut meat and potato into small dice. Season well. Make pastry as for short crust. Roll out thinly and cut into 8 rounds. Divide mixture into 8 portions, put on to each piece of pastry, damp edges round, fold over in half, crimp edge with finger and thumb. Glaze with beaten egg, prick top with fork. Bake in hot oven 15 minutes, then continue in a medium/slow oven to cook the meat and vegetables. Total time about 1 hour.

Note. Cooked meat and vegetables may be used if liked, when the cooking time is 20–25 mins. in a hot oven. The meat should be thoroughly reheated.

• COW-HEEL BROTH •

Put a cow-heel into a saucepan with three quarts of water, and set it to boil.

Skim it well and season with a few peppercorns, a sprig of thyme & parsley & a teapoonful of salt. Boil gently for two hours.

At the end of this time the broth will be reduced to half its original quantity.

Skim off the grease & serve the broth with the glutinous part of the heel in it.

• COW-HEEL AND BEEF •

1 cow-heel (cooked)	1 lb. shoulder steak
1 oz. dripping	$\frac{1}{2}$ oz. flour
1 onion	Pepper and salt
1 pint warm water	

Method: Cut the steak into neat pieces, mix the flour, pepper, and salt in a piece of paper, toss the steak, and fry in the hot dripping. Cut and slice the onion and allow to brown also. Add the water and cook for half an hour. Cut the cow-heel into small pieces, add this and cook for one hour. Add pepper and salt, and if not thick enough add a little flour or cornflour; stir till boiling. Very nutritious.

• HAM AND BACON •

HAM—Soak in cold water for 8–24 hours according to age and saltiness.

Scrape rind and underside. Put into pan of cold water—bring slowly to boiling-point, skim well and simmer the time required. If ham to be served cold leave in water until cool, remove, strip off rind and cover with raspings. If ham to be served hot, remove from water as soon as it is cooked and cover with glaze or raspings.

BACON—Soak for 1 hour in cold water and then proceed as for ham.

Use ham stock for vegetable soups but test for saltiness. Corner of ham about 3 lbs. may be baked in oven in crust. Make crust: 1–1$\frac{1}{2}$ lbs. flour, and water to mix. Cover ham all over. Allow 30 minutes to pound, plus 30 minutes.

• HASH •

Ingredients:

$\frac{1}{2}$ lb. of cold cooked meat (left from the joint)
$\frac{1}{2}$ oz. of dripping
$\frac{1}{2}$ tea-spoonful of thyme and marjoram
1 onion
1 dessert-spoonful of flour
$\frac{1}{4}$ pint of stock or water
Salt and pepper to taste

Method: Remove all meat from the bones, cut it into small pieces. Break up the bones and put them into a pan with cold water; simmer one hour; strain, add salt and pepper. Heat the dripping, slice the onion and fry to a nice brown in the dripping, sprinkle in the flour and herbs, stir in the stock or water by degrees, let boil a few minutes; then put in the meat and make it thoroughly hot.

• HASLET •

1 lb. pork steak
$\frac{1}{2}$ lb. stale bread
1 dessert spoonful powdered sage
$\frac{1}{2}$ teaspoonful pepper
1 teaspoonful salt
slightly less than $\frac{1}{2}$ pint water
$\frac{1}{4}$ lb. caul or apron fat (from the butcher)

Method: Put pork and bread through a mincing machine, add sage, pepper, salt and water, and mix thoroughly well. Soak the caul in cold water for 30 minutes before using. Wrap the mixture in the caul, making oval shape. Keep it thick and bake slowly 1$\frac{1}{2}$ hours. When cold this will be found delicious.

• HOT POT •

1$\frac{1}{2}$ lbs. lamb chops or 1lb. shoulder steak
3 lbs. potatoes
Water and seasoning
1 onion

Method: Wipe the beef and cut into pieces. If using lamb chops, leave whole. Peel and slice the potatoes and onion. Arrange a layer of potatoes in a deep dish, then meat and onion, then a layer of potatoes having rounded ends to the top. Add seasoning and water to come half way up. Brush the tops of the potatoes with dripping. Cover over with a well greased paper or lid. Put into a hot oven at first then reduce the heat and allow to cook for at least two hours, until the meat is tender.

The traditional dish in which this was made is brown earthenware, with curved sides, and a lid. If using lamb or mutton chops, they fit nicely into the curved sides of the pot.

• LENTIL SOUP •

4–6 ozs. lentils
1 small carrot, turnip and onion
1 stick celery
1$\frac{3}{4}$ pts. water or stock
$\frac{1}{4}$ pt. milk
1 oz. margarine or butter
1 oz. flour
Pepper and salt

Method: Wash the lentils and put into the pan with water or stock; onion and celery cut into thin slices, and carrot and turnip diced. Add seasoning, and boil gently until vegetables are tender, 1–1½ hours. Rub through a sieve. Melt the fat in the same pan, add the flour, mix well, and then add the milk, and lastly the sieved soup. Bring to boiling-point, stirring all the time; boil 3 or 4 minutes.

• LIVER AND BACON •

½ lb. lamb's liver	½ teaspoonful salt
¼ lb. bacon rashers	⅛ teaspoonful pepper
½ tablespoonful flour	¼ pt. stock

Wash liver in salted water, dry well. Cut into slices ¼ inch thick, removing skin. Coat with seasoned flour just before frying. Prepare bacon, remove rind, cut into medium-sized pieces. Heat pan, fry bacon, and put aside and keep hot. Fry liver in bacon fat, add a little more fat if necessary. Remove liver. *Make gravy:* Leave 1 teaspoonful of fat in pan, mix in remains of seasoned flour, brown, add stock, bring to boiling-point, boil 3 minutes; season. *To serve:* Place liver in centre of dish with piece of bacon on each piece. Strain thickened gravy round.

• MEAT (RAG) PUDDINGS •

These are often known as "Rag Puddings"—because they are cooked in a cloth.

½ lb. raw minced beef
1 small chopped onion
1 teaspoonful chopped parsley
Pinch of mixed herbs
Suet crust (made with 8 oz. flour etc.)
Seasoning
A little thick gravy

Mix beef, onion, herbs and seasoning with the gravy. It should not be too liquid. Roll out suet crust and spread meat mixture on it. Roll up, keeping the filling away from the edges, wrap in cloth previously dipped in boiling water and floured. Tie cloth both ends and put into boiling water. Boil 2 to 2½ hours. topping up the pan with <u>boiling</u> water, as necessary. Alternatively it may be steamed. Serve with brown sauce or gravy and vegetables.

• MEAT & POTATO PIE •
(INDIVIDUAL SIZE)

¼ lb. skirt or shoulder steak
½ lb. potatoes
Small piece of onion
Pepper & salt
Water half way up the dish

Method: Prepare 4 oz. pastry for the top of pie. Wipe & cut up meat. Dice the potatoes. Cut up the onion. Arrange the meat & vegetables in layers in the dish which must be well filled. Add seasoning and water HALF way up. Roll out pastry a little larger than the dish. Cut off trimmings to line the edge of dish. Wet the edge & put on lining. Wet the lining, put on the lid. Trim (cutting round outside edge) & decorate the edge and the top with pastry rose & leaves. Make a hole for the steam to escape. Put into a hot oven at first & when pastry has set reduce the heat to low & finish cooking slower. Small pie 1–1½ hrs.
N.B. A piece of greased paper on top of a pie will prevent it browning too much.

• MINT SAUCE (FRESH) •

¼ pint vinegar
1 tablespoonful sugar
2 tablespoonfuls chopped mint

Method: Wash and chop mint very finely, put vinegar into a sauce tureen, add sugar, and allow to dissolve; lastly, add mint. Serve with roast lamb.

• MINT SAUCE (PRESERVED) •

Chop mint fine, place in wide-mouthed bottle. Boil some vinegar, pour over mint, cork well. When needed take out the required quantity and sweeten. Nice for winter. Will keep good for months, even when often opened.

• MOCK DUCK •

Breast of mutton or lamb
Sage and onion stuffing
Thick brown gravy

Skin the mutton and remove the bones. Spread it with the stuffing. Roll it up and tie into shape.
Bake in plenty of good dripping, baste well and allow double the time you would for roasting. Serve with apple sauce and baked potatoes.

• PEA SOUP •

Nourishing and warm, this was a firm winter favourite, especially when made with stock in which bacon, ham or bacon ribs had been cooked. Sometimes a bacon or ham bone could be had from the grocer, and this was added to the soup during the cooking time.
Ordinary dried peas can be used, or split peas, (which don't have the rather indigestible shells of whole dried peas).

6 oz. dried peas or split peas. Soaked overnight.
Chop 1 large onion
2 large carrots
2 sticks celery (including the leaves if you have them)
1 small turnip
2 bay leaves

Fry the chopped vegetables gently in 1 tablesp. of oil or butter until soft, in a large saucepan.
Add 2 pints hot water or bacon stock, bacon bones or ribs (if used) and bay leaves.

Add pepper and salt as necessary (the latter may not be necessary if bacon stock is used, as that is salty).

Add the drained, soaked peas.

Bring to the boil, reduce to a simmer and simmer gently for 3–4 hours, or until the peas are cooked.

N.B. Split peas will only take about $1\frac{1}{2}$ hours. Check seasoning and serve very hot.

• POTATO CAKES (FRIED) •

Have some good mealy potatoes freshly boiled and mash 6 good-sized ones, adding a little salt until they are creamy and free from lumps. Then add sufficient good flour to make a dough that is easy to roll. Have the cakes cut from this about $\frac{1}{2}$ in. thick, and fry them, browning them on both sides on a hot girdle or in a frying-pan with a little good fat. When done split them, butter them generously and serve very hot.

• POTATO CAKES (BAKED) •

$\frac{1}{2}$ lb. cold mashed potato
$\frac{1}{2}$ lb. flour
4 ozs. cooking fat or lard
1 teaspoonful salt
$\frac{1}{2}$ teaspoonful baking powder

Mix potato, freed from lumps, with flour and rub in fat, add baking powder and salt. Roll out to $\frac{1}{2}$ inch thickness and cut in rounds with cutter. Bake 10 minutes in hot oven. Split open, spread with margarine or butter.

Potato cakes are at their best eaten immediately but are very good re-heated for breakfast in frying pan with bacon.

• POTATO PIE •

For 6 people:–

$1\frac{1}{2}$ lb. skirt or stewing steak, cut into cubes about 1"

8 large potatoes, peeled and cut into 1" cubes

2 large onions, chopped

Mix all ingredients and put into the potato pie dish. Add about 1 pt. hot stock (made with Oxo, Marmite or Bovril), salt and pepper to taste. Cover with foil.

Put into a medium oven approx. 325° for about $2\frac{1}{2}$ hours, when the meat should be tender. Take off the foil. Cover with a substantial shortcrust pastry "lid" and bake in a hot oven for about 20 mins. until brown.

Serve with pickled red cabbage or sliced beetroot in vinegar.

The best-known Lancashire dish, which could be made in any quantity, according to the size of the dish. Traditionally a dark brown high-sided dish was used. These dishes are still available, and are known locally as "potato-pie dishes." Potato-pie suppers were a popular event at church socials, and fund-raising events. Newly-baked potato pies would be donated to the event, and would be brought to the church hall wrapped in tea towels and a blanket to keep them warm until they could be put into an oven.

• POTTED HAM •

A piece of ham with an awkward bone running through it is extravagant if served in the usual way. It is possible to make it quite an economical dish by cooking it with an onion, carrot, peppercorn, etc., until the meat is just ready to slip from bone. Then take all the meat, fat, and lean, breaking it as little as possible, put into a mould, strain on to it a little of the stock in which it has been cooked and press with a heavy weight. When cold turn out.

• POTTED BEEF •

1 lb. best steak   Butter

Cut steak into small pieces, cook in double pan for 3 hours with 3 tablespoonful of cold water; add a piece of butter size of walnut, and seasoning to taste. Put twice through a mincer; place in small pots, cover with melted butter.

• PRESSED BEEF •

2- or 3-lbs. of brisket of beef, boned and rolled, removing skin. Place into a broad-bottomed basin with 3 tablespoonful of water and seasoning, tie over the top a buttered paper. Place in a large saucepan of water, to come half way up the basin, adding more as it boils away. Cook for 3½ hours, then uncover and skim grease from top. Place the meat on a dish, pour over the liquor, put a strong plate and flat iron on top, and leave until set. This will be found to be very tender and full of flavour. (If you do not have a flat-iron, use a heavy weight.)

• RABBIT CASSEROLE •

1 small rabbit
½ lb. tomatoes
¾ pint stock
2 ozs. dripping
1 large onion
½ bay leaf
Pepper and salt
2 small tablespoonfuls flour

Method: Wash and joint rabbit, toss this in flour, pepper and salt, and put into a casserole. Melt dripping in pan, fry sliced onion, add bay leaf and remaining flour, stir well, add skinned tomatoes and stock, stir till boiling, pour over rabbit, put into a slow oven and cook one and a half hours.

• SALMON PASTE •

Flake and mash a tin of salmon, remove the bones, use the liquid, add vinegar and ground mace to taste, melt 1 oz. butter, mix all together, press in pots and cover with more melted butter.
Makes tasty sandwiches.

• 'DUCK' HASH •

–using "savoury ducks"–economical and savoury.
From 1920's/1930's/wartime period.

Make a pan of potato hash as usual—potatoes, onions, carrots, stock—(but no meat).
Add savoury ducks when the vegetables are cooked.—They "melt down" and make hash thick and tasty.

• SAVOURY DUCKS •

Were made as follows:– Scraps of bacon, liver and other offal were minced and mixed with oatmeal, herbs (usually sage) and seasoning. Suet, bread

crumbs and onion were added. The mixture was shaped into balls, packed closely together in a baking tin, then baked in the oven.

Duck - a muffin stalls on Tommyfield Market sold a hot savoury duck on a muffin, with a thick gravy, and were probably one of the first "fast takeaway" foods.
The savoury ducks could be bought cold from butcher's shops and were often used for "Duck Hash"

• SCOTCH BROTH •

1 oz. pearl barley
8 ozs. scrag end neck of mutton
1 qt. water
Salt and pepper
2 teaspoonfuls chopped parsley
1 carrot ⎫
½ turnip ⎬ cut in dice
½ onion ⎪
1 stick celery ⎭

Method: Wash barley, remove fat from meat and cut in pieces, put meat into the water in a pan and soak for 15 minutes, then cook slowly for 1 hour. Skim fat off the broth, add the vegetables and seasoning and simmer 2 hours, skimming occasionally. Take out the meat, cut up a little into dice (about 2 tablespoonfuls), return to the pan and re-heat, taste, and add more seasoning if necessary. Free soup from all fat, pour into a hot soup tureen and sprinkle in the parsley.

• SHEEP'S HEAD, BOILED •

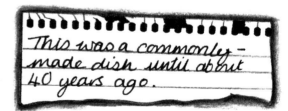

This was a commonly-made dish until about 40 years ago.

1 sheep's head   Pepper and salt
2 ozs. margarine   2 tablespoonfuls
2 ozs. flour   chopped parsley

| ½ pint milk | 1 teaspoonful |
| ½ pint stock | powdered sage |

Method: Remove all the soft bones near the nostrils of head, also take out the brain. Put the head and brain into a very large bowl of cold water and salt, and if possible leave to stand overnight, if not, for 2 hours, then wash the head thoroughly well in cold water. Put into a large pan, cover with cold water and allow to boil; cook slowly for 2½ to 3 hours. The brain can be put in about 1 hour before head is cooked. Take head out and cut all meat from the bones, skin the tongue and put all on to a hot dish, keep warm. Chop brain and parsley, melt margarine in pan, add flour and cook for a minute, add milk and stock (from cooking head). Stir till boiling, add pepper, salt, brain, sage and parsley and pour carefully over meat on dish. If not wishing to serve head hot, the meat can be chopped, pepper, salt, sage and a little butter added, and put into meat pots.

• SHIN OF BEEF CASSEROLE •

Comparatively few people realize how excellent and full of flavour is shin of beef, cooked in this way. This cut of meat, which contains much nourishment, needs long, slow cooking, and must never be browned. Choose the upper part of the shin and cut about 1 lb. of it into small pieces, removing all bone and skin. Put the meat into a casserole or stew-jar, season it with a little salt, not too much pepper and a dust of nutmeg, sprinkle it with 2 tablespoonfuls of vinegar (if liked)—this helps to soften the fibres of the meat—and pour in enough stock or water to just cover the meat. Put the lid on the casserole and cook slowly in the oven until tender.

• STEAK AND ONIONS •

1 lb. rump steak,	1 tablespoonful flour
(¾–1 inch thick)	1 teaspoonful salt
2–3 onions	⅛ teaspoonful pepper
2 ozs. dripping	¾ pt. stock or water

Method: Peel and slice onions in rings. Heat dripping, put in onions, cover with lid and cook 10 minutes until tender, remove lid and brown. Trim meat, beat with damp rolling-pin. Dip in seasoned flour. Remove onions, add more fat if necessary and fry meat, turning frequently. Cook 10–15 minutes. Remove meat. *Make Gravy:* Leave 1 tablespoonful dripping in pan, add remainder of seasoned flour, mix well and brown. Add stock or water. Bring to boil, boil 3 minutes, (add gravy browning if required). *To serve:* Put meat on hot dish, garnish neatly with onions and strain gravy round.

• OX TONGUE •

If you buy a brined tongue, ask the butcher how long he advises you to soak it. Probably 2–3 hours will be enough. If it is a smoked tongue, it will require 12 hours' soaking, as do most hams. If it is a fresh tongue, simply wash it.

To boil a brined tongue (a tongue pickled in a salt brine), first soak it for the required time, than place it in a stewpot with cold water to cover. Add a bouquet garni (parsley, small sprig of thyme and a small bay leaf) and bring slowly to the boil. Skim, then, for a large tongue, simmer for 3 hours or, for a smallish one, 2–2½ hours. Strain off enough stock to make a jelly.

Melt ¾ oz. best quality powdered gelatine to 1 pint stock. Taste and season sufficiently. Remove the tongue from the pot, skin it, remove any bones and trim it. Fit into a tongue mould or a similarly shaped shallow round dish, then fit in the trimmings to even out the shape. Pour the gelatine stock on the top and put in a cool place or refrigerator to set.

Often the tongue was placed without any liquid into a basin, a plate put on top with a heavy weight. The tongue would be left overnight in a cool place, and turned onto the serving dish next day.

• UNRATIONED MEAT DISHES •

• TRIPE AND ONIONS •

1lb. tripe
2 large onions
Salt and pepper
1 pint milk and water
1 oz. flour

Bring the onions to the boil, then slice thinly. Wash the tripe thoroughly and cut into pieces. Put the tripe and onions in a saucepan, season and cover with the milk and water. Simmer for two hours. Mix the flour to a smooth paste with a little milk, then stir this paste into the tripe and onions. Stir and boil for five minutes. Serve.

• WOOLTON PIE •

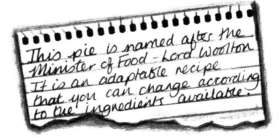

This pie is named after the Minister of Food – Lord Woolton. It is an adaptable recipe that you can change according to the ingredients available.

Cooking time: about 1 hour.

Dice and cook about ½ lb. of each of the following in salted water: parsnips, cauliflower, swedes, carrots, turnips. Strain, but keep ¾ pint of the vegetable water.

Arrange the vegetables in a large pie-dish or casserole. Add a little vegetable extract and about 1 oz. rolled oats or oatmeal to the vegetable liquid. Cook until thickened and pour over the vegetables: add 3–4 chopped spring onions.

Top with pastry or with mashed potatoes and cook in the centre of a moderately hot oven until golden brown.

• PUDDINGS & CAKES •

• BIBLE CAKE •

Mix together:–

12 oz.	I Kings 4:22	flour (plain)
8 oz.	Judges 5:25	butter
8 oz.	Jeremiah 6:20	cane sugar
6 oz.	I Samuel 25:18	raisins
6 oz.	Nahum 3:12	figs
3 oz.	Numbers 17:8	almonds (blanched and chopped)
1 tbs.	I Samuel 14:25	honey

Season to taste with:–

	II Chronicles 9:9	spices (mixed)
Add 3	Jeremiah 17:11	eggs
+ pinch	Leviticus 2:13	salt
¼ pt.	Judges 4:19	milk
1½ tsp.	Amos 4:5	leaven (baking powder)

Method:–
Solomon's prescription for the making of a good boy, Proverbs 23: 14 (Beat).
Bake in a moderate oven.

• BISCUIT CAKE •

8 oz. Marie biscuits
3 oz. marg.
1 tablesp. sugar
1 tablesp. cocoa
1 good tablesp. syrup
¼ lb. cooking chocolate or dessert chocolate

Break biscuits.
Melt marg., sugar, syrup & cocoa in pan. Mix in biscuits. Press firmly into greased, loose-bottomed tin.
Melt chocolate over hot water. Spread over top of cake. Leave overnight to set.

• BREAD AND BUTTER PUDDING •

6 thin slices bread and butter, with crusts removed
1 pint milk
2 eggs
2 oz. sugar
4 oz. currants
1 oz. candied peel (chopped)
Little grated lemon rind

Method: Layer the bread & butter, with the fruit in a greased pie-dish. Beat eggs, add sugar and grated lemon rind, also milk. Pour over bread, etc. Bake very slowly about one hour.
If the bread and butter is spread with either marmalade or raspberry jam, and the currants and peel omitted, an excellent pudding will be the result.

• CARAMEL CORNFLAKE CRUNCH •

3 oz. marg., 3 oz. sugar, 3 oz. syrup – MELT.

Add 4 tablesp. evaporated milk & boil until very soft caramel forms. Add 4 oz. cornflakes. Mix. Pour into shallow tin. Press. Leave to set. Cut into squares.

• CHRISTMAS PUDDING •

Makes 8 puddings
each serving 2–3 persons

8 oz. S.R. flour
8 oz. white breadcrumbs
8 oz. suet
8 oz. brown sugar
1 lb. mixed fruit
2 eggs
1 small grated carrot ⎫
1 small grated apple ⎬ If making only ½ recipe, still use this quantity of carrot, apple & potato
1 small grated potato ⎭
Juice & rind of lemon
2 tablespns. black treacle
1 teaspn. salt
1 teaspn. mixed spice
Brandy or sherry
Milk to mix

Mix all together in large bowl. Divide into small bowls. Steam 2 hrs. Put in freezer when cold. Steam 2 hrs. when required.

• COCONUT CRUNCH •

Mix together:
1 cup cornflakes
1 cup S.R. flour
1 cup dessicated coconut
½ cup sugar
2 dess. drinking chocolate

Melt 5 ox. marg.
Add to dry ingredients.
Spread in greased swiss roll tin. Bake at 360° for 20 mins.

• CURD CHEESE CAKES •

Method: Let some sour milk stand until quite thick, then strain through muslin, add to half a pint of curds a well-beaten egg, a tablespoonful fine sugar, half a teacupful fine currants, a small piece of butter, and a little nutmeg.

Line patty tins with pastry & nearly fill with the mixture. Bake until brown.

• CUSTARD PIE •

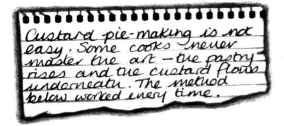

Custard pie-making is not easy. Some cooks never master the art – the pastry rises and the custard flows underneath. The method below worked every time.

Shortcrust pastry made with PLAIN flour and lard.
Line Pyrex dish with pastry.
Put on heated baking tray in oven at 375° for 10–15 mins.
Make custard with ½ pt. *hot* milk, 2 eggs, 1 tablespoon sugar, beaten together. Pour into pastry case.
Cook at 325° for 20–30 mins. or until the custard is set.
The top can be sprinkled with ground nutmeg.

• DRIPPING CAKE •

In a large pan put:–

    8 oz. dried fruit
    3 oz. dripping
    5 oz. sugar
    7½ fl.oz. water (large cupful)

Bring to the boil, simmer for 10 mins., then cool.
Sieve together:

    8 oz. plain flour
    Pinch salt
    1 tsp. baking powder
    ½ tsp. mixed spice
    ½ tsp. bicarbonate of soda

Add to the ingredients in the pan. Mix well. Put into a greased 6" tin and bake in a moderate oven (325°) for about 1¼ hrs., or until firm in the centre.

• DUMPLINGS •

    4 ozs. flour
    1½–2 ozs. suet* (chopped)
    ½ teaspoonful baking powder
    Pinch salt

Method: Mix the dry ingredients and add sufficient water to make a light dough. Divide into 8 or 10 and shape into balls. Cook in water 30–40 minutes* & serve with syrup or jam.

*Present-day commercially produced suet will have a shorter cooking time. Check on the packet.

• EGGLESS CAKE •

    4 oz. self-raising flour
    2½ oz. margarine

    3 oz. castor sugar
    Good pinch of salt
    1½ teaspoonfuls grated lemon rind
    2 oz. currants
    ¾ gill of milk (1 gill = ¼ pint)

Grease and flour a small cake tin, (about 6" diameter). Beat the margarine and sugar together until soft and creamy. Stir in the sieved flour and milk alternately. Lastly add currants, salt and lemon rind.
Stir thoroughly and put into prepared tin.
Bake for one hour, at 380°F.

• FLAT-CAKE (or FATTY CAKE) •

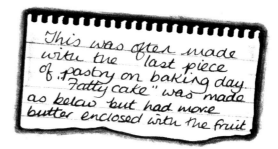

This was often made with the last piece of pastry on baking day. "Fatty cake" was made as below but had more butter enclosed with the fruit.

Roll out short-crust pastry to a circle. Into the middle put currants, raisins and sultanas (the combination as you like). Dot with butter and sprinkle generously with sugar. Fold the pastry from around the edge over to the middle. Dampen with water and press down, enclosing all the fruit and making sure the edges are sealed.
Put on a baking tray and flatten gently with a rolling pin.
Brush top with milk to brown it.
Bake in a medium-hot oven.
Serve cold, cut into wedges, spread with butter.

• FRUIT CAKE (RICH) •

YOU NEED:

    7 oz. plain flour
    Pinch salt
    ½ level teaspoon each mixed spice and cinnamon
    6 oz. best margarine
    6 oz. soft brown sugar
    1 tablespoon black treacle
    ½ teaspoon each vanilla and almond essences
    3 large eggs
    2 lb. mixed dried fruit, add 2 oz. glacé cherries
    2 tablespoons milk or sweet sherry

Method: Set the oven at 300°F or gas 2. Grease well a 7 in. round cake tin. Line base and sides with double thickness of greaseproof paper.
Sift dry ingredients on to large plate. Cream fat, sugar, treacle and essence together in large bowl until light and fluffy. Beat in whole eggs singly, adding tablespoonful of the dry mix with each.

Stir in fruit and cherries. Gently stir in rest of dry mix with sherry or milk. Spoon into tin. Smooth evenly with knife. Make shallow well in centre to stop cake doming.

Bake in oven centre 3 to 3½ hours, (covering with foil if top browns too much). Leave in tin ½ hour before turning out and cooling on wire rack. Store in airtight tin in a cool dry place.

This makes a good Christmas Cake.

• FRUIT CAKE ("EVERYDAY") •

6 oz. marg. ⎫ cream
6 oz. sugar ⎭
2 large eggs & little cold water to mix
8 oz. plain flour ⎫ sift and
3 level teasp. baking powder ⎭ fold in
8 oz. fruit (e.g. raisins, peel, cherries etc.)

Put into 7" tin. Bake 325°. Test with skewer to see if cooked after 45 mins. Bake until cooked.

• FRUIT CRUMBLE •

Crumble topping:–
    8 oz. flour
    2 oz. butter or margarine

Rub together.
Add 2 oz. sugar, and stir in.

Put 1 lb. fresh fruit—chopped apples, rhubarb, blackberries etc. into a greased pudding dish. Sprinkle with sugar (about 4 oz. per lb. of fruit). Top with crumble topping and dot with butter. Stand the dish on a baking sheet.

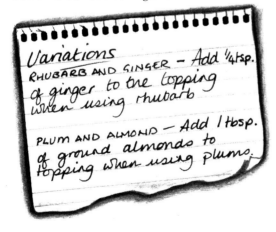

Variations
RHUBARB AND GINGER — Add ¼tsp. of ginger to the topping when using rhubarb

PLUM AND ALMOND — Add 1 tbsp. of ground almonds to topping when using plums.

Bake in a moderate oven until the fruit is cooked and the topping brown.

The exact timing depends on the type of fruit and the depth of the pie dish. Keep an eye on it after ½ hr., and test if the fruit is cooked by pushing a fork into the middle to feel if the fruit is soft.

• FRUIT SCONES •

8 oz. S.R. flour	1 egg
2 oz. marg.	Milk
1 oz. sugar	2 oz. dried fruit

Rub fat into flour. Add sugar & fruit. Beat egg & add to mixture, (saving a little for egg wash).
Gradually add milk to form soft dough. Roll to ½" thick. Cut out. Brush with egg. Bake at 450°–475° about 10 mins.

• GINGER BISCUITS •

3 oz. butter	7 oz. S.R. flour
3 oz. sugar	½ tsp. bi-carbonate of soda
1 egg	½ tsp. cream of tartar
1 dess. syrup	1 tsp. ground ginger

Cream butter & sugar—very soft. Add all dry ingredients, sifted together. Add syrup & egg to form paste. Roll into walnut-sized balls. Place on baking sheet. Bake for 10 mins. at 350°. Makes 36. *N.B.* They will spread when baking. Only put about 12 on a baking sheet.

• GINGERBREAD •

Sieve together:
    1 lb. plain flour
    2 tsp. ground ginger
    2 tsp. baking powder
    ½ tsp. bicarbonate of soda
    ½ tsp. salt

Warm gently together in a large pan until melted:
    8 oz. brown sugar
    6 oz. margarine or butter
    12 oz. syrup

Add:
    ½ pt. milk
    1 beaten egg
    and all the dry ingredients.

Mix thoroughly.
Pour into greased, lined baking tin.
Bake in a moderate oven (at 325°) for about 1½–1¾ hrs. or until the centre is firm to the touch.

• GINGER CRUNCH •

4 oz. soft brown sugar ⎫
3 oz. marg. ⎬ melt
2 oz. syrup ⎭
Add:
    6 oz. oats
    1 teasp. ground ginger

Turn into greased, 8" square tin. Smooth level. Bake for 25 mins. at 360°. Mark into fingers when cold.

• GIRDLE CAKES •

3 oz. marg. ⎫
8 oz. S.R. flour ⎬ Rub in
1½ oz. sugar ⎫
2 oz. currants ⎬ Stir in
Milk to mix into dough.

Roll out to just under ½" thick. Cut into rounds. Lightly grease griddle or heavy frying pan. Cook cakes over very low heat until golden brown on both sides & cooked through (10–15 mins).

• LIQUIDISER ALMOND CAKE •

4 oz. soft marg. ⎫
4 oz. sugar ⎪ Liquidise or beat
2 large eggs ⎬ together for 1 min.
6 tablesp. milk ⎭ (3 x 20 sec.)
6 oz. S.R. flour ⎫
1 dess. ground almonds ⎬ Sieve.
¾ level teasp. baking powder ⎭ Fold in.
Add:
4 oz. mixed fruit
1–2 oz. chopped nuts or
cherries (optional)

Pour into greased 7" tin. Smooth top. Bake in centre of oven, 350° for 1¼ hrs. or until firm.

• LANCASHIRE NUTS •

¼ lb. flour
¼ lb. butter
¼ lb. sugar
½ teaspoonful baking powder
¼ lb. cornflour
1 egg

Beat butter and sugar to a cream. Add egg and flour sifted with baking powder alternately. Shape into small round balls of an equal size. Flatten a little. Bake in a hot oven. When cold, put two together with lemon curd and dust with castor sugar.

• MADEIRA CAKE •

8 oz. flour (plain)
Pinch salt
1 tsp. baking powder
Finely grated rind of 1 lemon
5 oz. butter or margarine
5 oz. sugar
3 eggs
Milk to mix

Cream butter & sugar. Beat the eggs & add gradually to the creamed mixture, beating in. Fold in the sieved, dry ingredients, lemon rind and enough milk to give a soft, dropping consistency.
Put into a lined, greased tin.

Bake in a moderate oven 325° for about 1¼ hrs. or until firm to the touch.

• MALT LOAF •

¾ lb. self-raising flour   1 cup of milk
2 tablespoons malt   Salt
1 dessertspoon treacle
1 teaspoon bi-carbonate of soda
8 ozs. sultanas and currants (mixed)
2 tablespoons golden syrup
2 dessertspoons sugar

1. Warm milk, syrup, malt and bicarbonate of soda in saucepan.
2. Mix flour, salt, sugar and fruit in mixing bowl.
3. Stir in the warmed liquid.
4. Put into an oblong tin and bake in slow oven for 1¼ hours.

• MINCEMEAT •

½ lb. of apples
¼ lb. sugar
¼ lb. suet
¼ lb. currants
¼ lb. sultanas and raisins
2 ozs. peel
Rind and juice of lemon
Brandy to taste

Method: Chop apples, suet and peel, very finely, add well washed currants and raisins, add lemon juice and rind and sugar, mix very well, and add last of all brandy. Put in jars, wipe round tops of pots, and cover.

• ORANGE CAKE •

4 oz. marg.	1 teasp. baking pdr.
4 oz. sugar	1 orange rind (grated)
2 eggs	Juice ½ orange
4 oz. plain flour	

Cream butter & sugar.

Add well-beaten eggs, then flour & baking powder (sieved), then orange rind & juice. Put into greased tin. Bake at 350°, 20–30 mins. Ice with orange icing (made by using orange juice instead of water to mix).

• PARKIN •

In a large pan melt 3 oz. marg. and 3 oz. sugar. Add 1 cup milk. (Add 4 oz. S.R. flour, 4 ozs wholemeal flour, 4 oz. fine oatmeal.) Add 3 tablesp. syrup (good ones) and 1 good dess. black treacle. Sift dry ingredients (above in brackets) with 1 teasp. bicarb. & ¼ teasp. salt. Add to pan. Stir. Put in greased, lined tin. Bake *very* slowly. Mine was in 4 hours, sometimes only on 100°, but generally at 150°—it was just started at 225°.

• GRANNY'S PARKIN •

½ lb. S.R. flour
¼ lb. fine oatmeal
3 oz. sugar ⎫
3 oz. marg. ⎬ Rub into ↑
1 teasp. bicarb. ⎫
¼ tsp. salt ⎬ Add
3 tablesp. syrup
1 teacup warm milk ⎭

Put into greased, lined tin (about 7" square). Bake 1 hr. 20 mins., slow oven.

• QUEEN OF PUDDINGS •

2 ozs. breadcrumbs	1 oz. margarine
2 eggs	A little jam
½ pt. milk	2 oz. sugar

Method: Beat up the yolks of the eggs with 1 oz. sugar. Make the milk hot in a pan & add to it the margarine. Pour the hot milk on to the egg. Return all to the pan & slightly cook. Pour over the breadcrumbs. Put this mixture into a pie dish & bake in a moderately hot oven until it sets. Spread over the top with jam and pile on the top the stiffly whipped white of egg to which has been added 1 oz. Sugar. Return to the oven to brown and set.

• RICE PUDDING •

This was often cooked in the same oven as the Hot Pot or other dishes requiring long, slow cooking.

Put 1½ oz. round grain rice into a pie dish. Add 1 tbsp. sugar, and 1 pint milk.
Dot surface with butter, and sprinkle with ground nutmeg (if liked).
Bake in a slow oven (300°F) for 2 hours.

• ROCK CAKES •

½ lb. flour
3 ozs. currants
3 ozs. sugar
1 oz. candied peel
One teaspoonful of baking powder

Rub all together and mix to a moderately stiff dough with milk. Drop on greased paper with a fork in little heaps so that the surface has a rough uneven appearance. Bake quickly in a hot oven to a light brown. For laying by, 4 ozs. of butter should be added to the other ingredients, and a beaten egg can be used to mix the dough.

• ROLY POLY PUDDING •

SERVE WITH WHITE OR CUSTARD SAUCE.

¼ lb. flour
2 oz. suet
¼ teaspoonful of salt
¼–½ teaspoonful baking powder
Water to mix
Jam

Method: Mix flour, salt, suet, baking powder. Add water to make a stiff paste. Roll out on a floured board. Spread on jam to ½" of edge. Wet the edge and roll up. Tie in a floured and scalded cloth.
Small Pudding – Boil ¾ hour.
Large Pudding – Boil 1½ hours.

• RUSSIAN SANDWICH •

4 ozs. margarine	2 eggs
4 ozs. sugar	4 ozs. S.R. flour

Method: Cream butter and sugar. Add eggs separately. Add flour and baking powder, mix well. Bake in moderate oven 40 minutes.

Filling for Russian Sandwich

½ pt. milk	1 oz. cornflour
1 egg	1½ oz. castor sugar
Few drops vanilla essence	

Mix sieved cornflour with sugar and egg. Heat milk, pour onto mixture, mix very well. Return to saucepan and bring to boil, stirring all the time. Boil gently for 2 mins. until thickened. Remove from heat. Add vanilla essence to taste.
Split cake open and spread the filling. Cover top of cake with water icing. Decorate outer edge of cake (for about 1 inch) with dessicated coconut.

• SHORTBREAD •

2 oz. sugar   6 oz. flour (plain)
4 oz. butter

Rub fat into flour. Add sugar. Knead. Press into 7"
tin. Bake at 325° until golden. Mark into pieces.

• SYRUP TART •

Line a greased pie-dish with shortcrust pastry (6 oz.
pastry for 8" plate).
Put 2 oz. fresh breadcrumbs into a bowl with 6 oz.
warmed syrup and the juice of $\frac{1}{2}$ lemon. Mix together,
then spread onto the pastry, spreading evenly.
Brush the edges of the pastry with milk, to brown.
Bake at 400°F for about 20 mins.

• TEA LOAF •

Soak $\frac{3}{4}$ lb. dried fruit & $\frac{1}{4}$ lb. brown sugar in $7\frac{1}{2}$ fl.oz.
strained cold tea. Leave overnight. Next day, stir in
$\frac{1}{2}$ lb. self-raising flour, 1 egg, 1 teasp. mixed spice.
Bake 375° for 1–1$\frac{1}{2}$ hrs.
Serve sliced, with butter.

Variation: Add 3–4 oz. chopped nuts, dot with butter
& sprinkle with sugar before baking.

• TREACLE LAYER PUDDING •

Roll out a piece of suet crust and cut into rounds.
Have ready some golden syrup that has been
warmed and thickened with breadcrumbs and
flavoured with lemon juice. Well grease a basin and
line it with a piece of the pastry, put in some of the
treacle mixture and then a piece more pastry. Repeat
the process until the basin is full, cover the top with
a piece of suet crust and bake in a moderate oven.

• TRIFLE •

Large swiss roll
Tin of strawberries or raspberries
Glass (or two) of sherry
1 pt. thick custard
Whipped cream

Slice the swiss roll and put into the bottom of a glass
bowl. Pour over it the sherry, and the tin of fruit,
including all the juice.
Pour 1 pint of custard over that. Allow to cool and
set.

Top with whipped cream.
Decorate with cherries and flaked almonds.

• WAKES CAKE •

$\frac{1}{2}$ lb. plain flour   1 oz. currants
Pinch salt   1 egg well beaten
6 ozs. butter or margarine   Milk to mix
6 ozs. sugar

Sieve the flour and salt rub in the fat then add the
sugar and fruit. Mix to a stiff dough with egg,
adding a little milk if necessary. Knead, put on a
floured board, roll out and cut in rounds the size of
a saucer. Bake in a moderate oven till light golden,
& sprinkle sugar on top before serving. These cakes
are traditionally eaten during the Wakes (holiday)
week.

• WHOLEMEAL BISCUITS •

1 cupful wholemeal flour
1 cupful demerara sugar
1 cupful porridge oats
A few raisins

Melt in pan to golden brown—
4 ozs. butter
1 small teaspoonful bicarbonate of soda
1 dessertspoonful treacle
2 dessertspoonfuls boiling water

Mix with dry ingredients and drop in spoonful on
baking sheet. Bake in oven, Regulo 6, 15 minutes.

• MISCELLANEOUS •
(PRESERVES & DRINKS)

• BRAMBLE JELLY •

Blackberries
Sugar
Water

Gather blackberries that
are not too ripe. Put them
into a preserving pan and
nearly cover with cold
water. Bring to boil,
simmer one hour.
Crush fruit with wooden
spoon to extract juice. Strain through jelly bag,
muslin or hair sieve. Leave to drain all night.
Next day measure juice. Allow $\frac{3}{4}$ lb. sugar to 1 pint
of juice. Put sugar in the oven to warm. Boil juice 15
minutes, then add warmed sugar. Boil till it jellies;
this point is reached when a little of the syrup sets
quickly when tested on a cold plate.

• BLACKCURRANT JAM (MICROWAVE) •

Wash 1 lb. blackcurrants.
Put in very large bowl with ½ pt. water (boiling).
Microwave 10 mins. covered. Stir twice.
Warm 1 lb. 3 oz. sugar.
Add to fruit, with 4 tablesp. boiling water.
Continue with the bowl uncovered.
Microwave 7 mins., stirring twice, until sugar dissolved.
Microwave 20 mins. (Have cold plate ready to test for set.)
Made 2 lbs.

Have also done this with elderberries—very good (and free).

• MARMALADE •

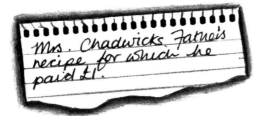

Mrs. Chadwicks Father's recipe for which he paid £1.

Take six bitter Seville oranges, three sweet oranges and one lemon. Cut them in quarters and take out all the pips. Then shred them altogether both insides and peel according to taste, fine or coarse. When cut up weight the whole and to every pound add three pints of water. Put it by in a bowl to steep for 24 hours. Then boil the whole for half an hour and put it by again for 24 hours to steep.
Then add 1½ lbs. of lump sugar to every pound of fruit and liquid & boil it half an hour and it will be ready for putting in pots.

• QUICK ORANGE MARMALADE •

2 pts. water	4 lb. sugar
2 lb. oranges	Juice 2 lemons•

Halve the oranges (after washing).
Remove pips & put in muslin. Without soaking, pressure-cook for 25–30 mins., at 15 lb. pressure. Remove pips. Mash fruit with potato masher. Add sugar, lemon juice, & stir until dissolved. Boil in open cooker until a little sets on cold plate. Pour into warm jars and seal in usual way. 5–6 lb. yield.

Have made GRAPEFRUIT marmalade, as above, very successfully.

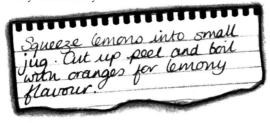

Squeeze lemons into small jug. Cut up peel and boil with oranges for lemony flavour.

• LEMON CURD •

Grate the rind of 1 large lemon into a bowl. Add 3 oz. castor sugar.
Whisk 2 large eggs with the juice of the lemon, then pour this over the sugar.
Add 2 oz. butter, cut into small pieces.
Put the bowl over a pan of *gently* simmering water.
Stir frequently until thick (probably 20–30 mins.).
Put into small pots and cover.

• CHUTNEY •

2 lbs. apples
2 lbs. sugar
¼ lb. salt
¼ lb. mustard seeds
1 lb. raisins
1 lb. onions
1 dessertspoonful ground ginger
½ teaspoonful cayenne
1 pint vinegar

Chop apples and onions very finely. Boil apples in vinegar. Dissolve sugar and salt in remainder of vinegar, and add onions and other ingredients to apples, and boil for a further 15 to 20 minutes. If preferred, onions, apples and raisins may be put through the mincer. Pour into jars and seal when cold.

• BARLEY WATER •

2 ozs. pearl barley
1 quart water
Little salt
Strip lemon rind

Method: Wash barley and put into a pan with salt water and lemon rind, allow to boil and simmer slowly for two hours. Strain and use as required.

• ELDERFLOWER CHAMPAGNE •

5 or 6 heads elderflowers
2 tbsp. white wine vinegar
2 lb. white sugar
8 pts. cold water
4 pts. hot water
2 lemons

Pick heads in full bloom. Put into bowl with vinegar, cut-up lemon rind & juice, & sugar dissolved in hot water. Add cold water & leave for 3 days, occasionally giving a good stir. Strain into strong bottles, cork firmly & lay on their sides. After about 2 weeks it should be sparkling and ready to drink.

• GINGER WINE •

Ginger Wine Essence	Drachms	Metric
Strong tincture of ginger	$2\frac{1}{2}$	8.5 ml
Tincture of capsicum	1	3.5 ml.
Essence of lemon	1	3.5 ml.
Solution of burnt sugar	2	7 ml.

Dissolve $1\frac{1}{2}$ lb. sugar in 4 pints boiling water. Allow to cool. Add essence as above, + $\frac{1}{2}$ oz. TARTARIC ACID. Bottle.

• A darker wine can be made by using more burnt sugar solution. *8 drachms or 28 ml. gives a very dark wine.)

• LEMONADE •

3 lemons
$1\frac{1}{2}$ lb. sugar
1 pt. water
1 oz. tartaric acid

1. Thinly peel lemons. Put into bowl with juice.
2. Make syrup with water & sugar.
3. Pour over rind & juice. Leave overnight.
4. Add 1 oz. tartaric acid. Stir until dissolved.
5. Bottle.
6. Serve diluted.

❏

UKRAINIAN DISHES

• KHRUSTY •

(Dainties)

3 eggs + 2 egg yolks
1 oz. sugar
1 tablesp. double cream
$\frac{1}{2}$ teasp. salt
1 tablesp. rum or brandy (optional)
1 lb. sifted self-raising flour
Icing sugar

Beat all the eggs until frothy and light. Add sugar, cream, salt, brandy/rum (if used). Fold in flour to make a soft dough. Knead lightly. Cover and set aside for 10 minutes. Using a small amount of dough (keeping the rest covered) roll out thinly. Cut into strips about $1\frac{1}{4}$ inches wide, then cut those strips into 3 inch lengths. Slit each piece in the centre, then pull one end through it to form a "knot". Cover until all the dough is shaped. Fry in deep oil, a few at a time, until lightly brown. Drain on kitchen paper, and dust with icing sugar.

• BORSCH •

(Beetroot soup)

$1\frac{1}{2}$ lb. shin of beef
4 pints cold water
1 teasp. salt
1 medium onion, diced
2 beetroot (uncooked), shredded finely
1 carrot, shredded finely
2 sticks celery, sliced
8 oz. cabbage, shredded finely
1 potato, diced
4 oz. diced green beans
$\frac{3}{4}$ pt. tomato juice or small tin tomatoes
Small clove garlic (optional)
1 tablespoon flour
Juice of $\frac{1}{2}$ lemon
Salt and pepper to season
Chopped fresh dill (or dried if fresh not available)
Cream or sour cream (when serving)

Cover the meat with the water, add salt, bring to the boil and simmer gently for $1\frac{1}{2}$ hrs. Remove any scum. Add onion, beetroot, carrot, celery, potato and green beans, and cook until vegetables are tender (about 25 mins.). Add the shredded cabbage and cook for about 5 mins. (do not overcook). Add tomato juice or tomatoes and garlic (if used). Thicken with flour. Add lemon juice. Season to taste. Add chopped dill. Just before serving, add the cream or sour cream, or serve separately.

• KHOLODETS •

(Jellied pigs feet)

3 pigs feet
$1\frac{1}{2}$ lb. pork shank
1 tablesp. salt
1 medium onion ⎫
2 sticks celery ⎬ leave whole
1 carrot ⎭
1 clove garlic
$\frac{1}{4}$ tsp. black peppercorns
2 bay leaves

The pigs feet are prepared by burning off any hairs over a gas ring, then scraping, trimming and washing very thoroughly. Chop the feet into two, lengthwise. In a large pan place the feet and the washed shank, cover with cold water, bring to the boil and skim. Simmer very gently for 3 hours. Add vegetables, garlic, peppercorns and bay leaves. Simmer until the meat is falling from the bone (probably another 2–3 hours). Take the meat from the pan, cut up the large pieces and put into a dish. Strain the broth and pour over the meat. Chill thoroughly, when it will form into a jelly. Remove any fat from the top. Serve cut into slices.

• VARENYKY •
(Filled Dumplings)

1 lb. self-raising flour
1 teasp. salt
1 beaten egg
4 fl.oz. (or more) water
Potato and cheese filling (next recipe)

Sift flour and salt. Add beaten egg and water to make a medium-soft dough. Knead lightly. Set aside for 10 minutes, whilst filling is prepared.

Roll out the dough on a floured board until quite thin. Cut into large rounds with a biscuit cutter, or into 2½-inch squares. Put a spoonful of filling on each round or square, and fold over to form a semi-circle or triangle shape. Press the edges together to make a good seal.

Have a large pan of boiling, salted water. Drop the varenyky (only a few at a time) into the water and cook for 3 or 4 minutes, until well puffed up. Drain thoroughly. Cover and keep warm until all cooked (coat with a little melted butter to keep from sticking together). Serve in a large dish, with smetana (sour cream) and/or crisp bacon.

Varenyky are some-what similar to Italian ravioli.

• CHEESE AND POTATO FILLING •
(For Varenyky).

8 oz. cold mashed potato
4 oz. cottage cheese (or grated Cheddar cheese, or cream cheese)
1 small onion
2 oz. butter
Salt and pepper

Finely chop the onion and fry gently (until softened) in the butter. Add the potato and cheese. Season to taste. Mix thoroughly.

• HOLUBTSI •
(Cabbage rolls)

Cabbage rolls may be prepared with a variety of fillings, and the liquid used for cooking may be water, stock or tomato juice.

1 head of cabbage
½ pt. tomato juice
1 oz. melted butter
Salt and pepper
¼ pt. sour cream
Meat and rice filling (next recipe)

Remove the hard central core from the cabbage. Cover the cabbage completely with boiling water and leave for a few minutes until the leaves become pliable. Take the leaves off one by one. Remove the hard stalk from each leaf. Place a good spoonful of filling on each leaf, and form into a parcel. Arrange these parcels (or rolls) in the cooking pot in layers. Mix together tomato juice, sour cream, butter and seasoning. Pour the liquid over the rolls, cover tightly (this is important) and bake for 1½–2 hours until cabbage and filling are cooked. Serve hot. Garnish with sour cream or chopped bacon.

• MEAT AND RICE FILLING •
(For Holubtsi)

8 oz. cooked rice
4 tablesp. oil
8 oz. minced beef
8 oz. minced pork } or 1 lb. minced beef
1 beaten egg
Salt and pepper
1 medium onion (chopped)

Soften the onion in the oil. When tender, add the minced meat and cook until lightly browned, stirring all the time. Remove from heat. Add the rice. Stir well. Add the beaten egg and season to taste.

• KUROCHKY •
(WEDDING BREAD DECORATIONS)

"Kurochky" translated means "chicks". These are made out of a special bread dough, so they will not lose their shape and then are placed on top of the traditional wedding cake (the "Korovay").

½ lb. strong plain flour
3 tablespoons cooking oil
6–9 tablespoons water (quantity variable according to the type of flour used)
1–2 tablespoons sugar (optional)

Mix all ingredients together to form a dough (roughly the same texture as for a pie).
Use two small pieces to make the chick.
Roll one piece into a small ball to form the body of a chick.
Roll the other piece into the shape and length of your finger. This piece will be used for the head and the tail.
To form the head make a knot in the finger shape;

attach to the body and form a beak. There should still be enough left from the head to mould the tail feathers and attach to the other end of the body. Mark the tail with a knife and insert peppercorns or currants to form the eyes. Brush with egg yolk and bake (350 °F or Gas Mark 4) for about 10 minutes, or until they become golden.

Microwave Method
If baking the "Kurochky" in a microwave, to the above ingredients half an egg needs to be added. There is then no need to brush the Kurochky with egg before baking.

□

• ASIAN RECIPES •

• AUBERGINE CURRY •
(Serves 4)

2 large aubergines
2½ teaspoons turmeric powder
Salt
Oil for frying

Curry:
¼ pt. milk (coconut milk or fresh milk)
¼ teaspoon chilli powder (optional)
Pinch turmeric powder
2 dessertspoons vinegar
1 onion very finely chopped
2 cloves garlic finely chopped
1 green chilli chopped (discard seeds for less hot effect)
1 tomato sliced (skinned if you prefer)

Utensils: frying pan, saucepan, mixing bowl.

Method: Slice the aubergines lengthwise and marinate them for about 15 minutes in salt and turmeric powder. Fry in batches until crisp and golden brown. Keep on one side.
Mix all the ingredients for the curry and bring to boil slowly on a gentle heat. When mixture thickens, add fried aubergine and cook for a few more minutes.

• CHAPATIS •
(Serves 4)

8 oz. wholewheat flour
Pinch of salt
About ¼ pt. water

Sieve the flour and salt into a bowl, and add about half the water. Mix into a dough. Knead for 15 mins. Add the remainder of the water and knead again for about 5–10 mins.

Leave to rest for 30 mins. Divide the dough into 12 portions. On a floured board, roll the dough into circles, 6 inches in diameter, and about ⅛" thick. In a pre-heated, oiled frying pan (or on a griddle), cook the thin circles of dough one at a time, on both sides, until lightly brown and risen.
Chapatis may be frozen. Uncooked ones should be layered between sheets of freezer paper. They should be thawed and cooked as above. Cooked chapatis need not be thawed. If placed under a hot grill this will thaw and reheat them.

• FRIED ONION •
(Serves 4)

Served as an accompaniment to rice and curry.

2 large onions, cut into rings
1 green chilli, finely chopped (optional)
1 teasp. curry powder
¼ teasp. cumin seed
1 bay leaf
Salt and freshly ground pepper
Lemon or lime juice
Oil for frying

Heat oil in a frying pan. Add bay leaf and cumin seed. When cumin seed begins to darken in colour, add onions, chilli and curry powder. Cook on gentle heat, uncovered, until onions are soft. Season with salt, pepper and add lemon or lime juice to taste. Serve very hot.

• LENTIL CURRY •
(Serves 4)

8 oz. red lentils
½ pt. milk (coconut or fresh milk)
1 onion finely chopped
1 green chilli finely chopped
¼ teaspoon turmeric powder
Salt
Oil for frying
1 dried red chilli (optional)

Utensils: Bowl for soaking, saucepan, frying pan.

Method: Wash the lentils and soak them in milk for about two hours. Add ½ the onion, the chilli, turmeric powder and salt. Mix well and cook over a low heat. When the lentils are soft and golden in colour, fry them with the remainder of the onion and a dried red chilli if desired.

LENTIL AND SPINACH CURRY
Cook as above using all the onion. When the lentils are half cooked, add 2 oz. spinach, coarsely chopped. Omit the final stage of frying.

• MEAT CURRY •
(Serves 4)

1½ lbs. meat (lamb or beef) cubed
10 fl.oz. plain yoghurt (2 small cartons)
2 onions finely chopped
3 bay leaves
1 stick sweet cinnamon
3 cloves garlic
5 cloves
4 medium sized potatoes, boiled and diced
2 tablespoons tomato puree
½ dessertspoon ground cumin seed
1 teaspoon chilli powder
3 teaspoons curry powder
Salt
Lemon juice
Oil for frying

Utensils: Bowl, heavy saucepan with lid.

Method: Marinade the meat for 3 hours (or overnight in the fridge) in salt, curry powder, chilli powder and yoghurt.
Fry onions but do not brown them, together with the cinnamon, garlic cloves and bay leaves. Add meat and simmer, covered, for about ten minutes until the juices reduce. Add ½ cup water and diced potatoes. Cook on low heat for about 20 minutes, until the meat is tender. Next add the tomato puree and the ground cumin. If the gravy needs thickening, add 2 dessertspoon butter. Finally add lemon juice and salt to taste.

• ONION AND SPINACH PAKORAS •
(Serves 4)

8 oz. gram flour
¼ teasp. baking powder
1 teasp. salt
¼ teasp. coriander seeds, crushed
¼ teasp. ground ginger
¼ teasp. ground cumin
Water to mix (about ½ pint)
Oil for frying
Onions
Spinach. The proportion as you wish*

Cut the onions and spinach into small pieces, and set aside. Sieve the dry ingredients into a bowl and add enough water to make a thick batter (like a thick pancake batter).
Add the vegetables.
Heat the oil in a deep pan. Put 1 dessertspoonful of batter mixture at a time into the hot oil. Cook until golden brown (3–5 mins.). Drain on kitchen paper and serve immediately.

*Other vegetables may be used, either singly or combined. Potatoes, broccoli, aubergines, mushrooms or cauliflower are suggestions.

• SPICY CHICKEN LIVER •
(Serves 4)

1 lb. chicken livers
½ tsp. cumin seed
¼ tsp. chilli powder or 1 small green chilli, finely chopped
¼ tsp. coriander powder
1 large onion, chopped
1 large tomato (peeled if preferred), chopped
2 cloves garlic
1 piece fresh ginger root, (½" long)
1 bay leaf
2 cloves
Salt and freshly ground pepper
Oil for frying
2 oz. coriander leaf (optional), chopped

Fry onions until lightly browned, with the bay leaf, garlic, ginger and cumin seed. Add livers, chilli powder, cloves and coriander powder. Cook on a low heat until liver is soft but retains its shape. Now add tomato and coriander leaf. Cook, covered, for about 5 more minutes. Season to taste. Discard cloves, bay leaf and ginger root before serving. Serve very hot.

• SWEET ALMOND PUDDING •
(Serves 6)

1 small tin evaporated milk
4 oz. ground almonds
1 oz. soft brown sugar

Make up evaporated milk to 1 pint with water. Bring to the boil. Lower the heat. Add almonds and brown sugar, then simmer gently, stirring all the time until a creamy consistency is achieved.
Serve hot or cold.

• SWEET CARROT HALVA •

1 lb. peeled carrots
1½ pts. milk
5 oz. sugar
2½ oz. unsalted butter
1 oz. sultanas
1 dess. golden syrup

Grate the carrots finely and add the milk.
Cook gently in a heavy-bottomed pan, stirring regularly, until the mixture becomes almost solid. (*Note*: This may take up to 1 hour.)
Then add the syrup, butter, sugar and sultanas. Mix well. Return to a low heat. Stir continuously until the mixture begins to leave the sides of the pan. (This could take up to 20 mins.)
Spread the mixture into a buttered dish. Decorate with nuts or dried fruit if wished. Serve hot or cold. This is decorated with edible silver leaf for special occasions.